The History of Ancient Egypt
Part III

Professor Bob Brier

THE TEACHING COMPANY ®

PUBLISHED BY:

THE TEACHING COMPANY
4840 Westfields Boulevard, Suite 500
Chantilly, Virginia 20151-2299
1-800-TEACH-12
Fax—703-378-3819
www.teach12.com

ISBN 1-56585-622-8

Bob Brier, Ph.D.

Professor of Egyptology, Long Island University

Bob Brier was born in the Bronx, where he still lives. He received his bachelor's degree from Hunter College and Ph.D. in philosophy from the University of North Carolina at Chapel Hill in 1970.

From 1981–1996 he was Chairman of the Philosophy Department at C.W. Post campus of Long Island University and now primarily teaches Egyptology courses. He was Director of the National Endowment for the Humanities' Egyptology Today Program and has twice been selected as a Fulbright Scholar. He is also the recipient of the David Newton Award for Teaching Excellence.

In 1994, Dr. Brier became the first person in 2,000 years to mummify a human cadaver in the ancient Egyptian style. This research was the subject of a National Geographic television special, *Mr. Mummy*. Dr. Brier is also the host of The Learning Channel's series *The Great Egyptians*.

Professor Brier is the author of *Ancient Egyptian Magic* (Morrow: 1980), *Egyptian Mummies* (Morrow: 1994), *Encyclopedia of Mummies* (Facts on File: 1998), *The Murder of Tutankhamen: A True Story* (Putnam's: 1998), *Daily Life in Ancient Egypt* (Greenwood: 1999), and numerous scholarly articles.

Table of Contents
The History of Ancient Egypt
Part III

The History of Ancient Egypt

Scope:

There is something about ancient Egypt that fascinates almost everyone. Egyptian exhibits at museums draw the largest crowds, mummy movies pull in the largest audiences, and Egypt attracts the most tourists. Part of the attraction is undoubtedly the exotic nature of the beast. Treasures hidden in tombs seem always just around the corner; hieroglyphs, while beautiful, seem impossible to read; and the beautiful sculptures and paintings seem from a time incredibly long ago. In a sense, one goal of this course is to demystify ancient Egypt but not to take the fun out of it.

As we learn more and more about Egypt, it will all become familiar. Students will have an idea of how hieroglyphs work and what they say; we will come to know how archaeologists, using scholarship and learning, search for undiscovered tombs; and we will learn the techniques used to create the art of ancient Egypt. But as we learn more and more, the student should become more and more amazed by the culture. What was created on the banks of the Nile was an event unique in human history. No civilization lasted so long, contributed so much, or repeatedly amazed as did ancient Egypt.

Because Egyptian history lasted so long, Egyptologists divide it into three periods called *Kingdoms*: (1) The Old Kingdom saw the beginnings of nationhood for Egypt under one supreme ruler, the pharaoh. During this period, the pyramids were built, and the rules of Egyptian art were established that would govern for 3,000 years. (2) The Middle Kingdom, a period of stabilizing after the Old Kingdom collapsed, saw a nation fighting to regain its greatness. (3) The New Kingdom, the glamour period of ancient Egypt, was when all the stars—Hatshepsut, Tutankhamen, Ramses the Great, and others—appeared.

We will chronologically survey the full 3,000 years of recorded ancient Egyptian history, emphasizing that the ancient Egyptians were people just like ourselves, motivated by the same fears, doubts, and hopes. By the end of the course, students should feel that they know the kings and queens who made Egypt great. As we study the different reigns, we will also discuss various aspects of Egyptian civilization so that you should learn far more than just the rulers of ancient Egypt. You should be able to walk through the Egyptian collection of a museum and tell when a statue was carved, have an idea which pharaoh it is by the way the face is carved, and perhaps even be able to read the hieroglyphs to discern the king's name. In short, I want to turn out "junior Egyptologists," people with a deep understanding of Egypt, for whom ancient artifacts will not all look the same.

To a great extent, the fun of history is in the details. Knowing what kind of wine Tutankhamen preferred makes him come alive. Knowing that Ramses the Great was crippled by arthritis for the last decade of his long life makes us more sympathetic to the boastful monarch who fathered more than 100 children. If we understand what it was like to be a miner sent to the turquoise mines in the Sinai in the summer, we will feel a kinship with our long dead counterparts. As we wind our way chronologically through 30 centuries of history, we will pause repeatedly to look at the details that make up the big picture.

The first five lectures will really be a prolegomena. We will see what Egypt was like before writing, and we will learn how Egyptologists piece together the history of ancient Egypt. We will see how we know what we know—how hieroglyphs were deciphered, for example—and we will see that since then, Egyptology has been one ongoing detective story.

In Lectures Six through Ten, we will see the Egyptians rise to a greatness far surpassing any other people in the Near East. We learn of a king who united Egypt by might and of a pharaoh who showed Egypt how to build the pyramids. While we see how the pyramids were built, we will learn just what it was that made Egypt great. At the end of these lectures, we will see Egypt collapse into a dark age about which little is known, and we will try to figure out what happened.

Lectures Eleven through Sixteen discuss Egypt's successful attempt to pull itself together, only to collapse once again. We see heroic kings from the south battle to unite the country and establish a peace that would last for two centuries—as long as the United States has existed. Then we will see Egypt invaded by the mysterious people called the Hyksos, only to watch as the kings of the south battle Egypt back to greatness. We will also look in detail at the Old Testament story of Joseph in Egypt to see what light it might shed on this period.

Lectures Seventeen through Twenty-Five deal with the fabulous Dynasty XVIII, the period of Egypt's greatest wealth and personalities. We will take in-depth looks at the kings and queens of this period. We will see Hatshepsut, the woman who ruled as king; Akhenaten, the first monotheist in history, who changed the religion of Egypt; and Tutankhamen, the son of Akhenaten, who became the most famous of Egypt's kings when his undisturbed tomb was discovered in 1922.

Lectures Twenty-Five through Twenty-Eight are a brief excursion into my specialty, mummies. We will talk about everything you ever wanted to know about mummies, including how to make one. We will also see that mummies are like books—packed with information—if you know how to read them.

Lectures Twenty-Nine through Thirty-Five focus on the end of the New Kingdom, the last great epoch of Egyptian history. Dominated by Ramses the Great, this period also had other important kings, and we will discuss who was the unnamed pharaoh of the Exodus.

In Lectures Thirty-Six through Forty-One, we will see Egypt's greatness slipping away. Egypt will be invaded by a series of conquering peoples, including Nubians, Libyans, and Persians. It is a sad story, and we will examine the causes of Egypt's decline.

Egypt's last gasp is under the Greek kings, the Ptolemies. This period begins with the conquest of Alexander the Great and ends with Cleopatra. For 200 years, once mighty Egypt is ruled by kings named Ptolemy, all descended from General Ptolemy who served under Alexander. In Lectures Forty-Two through Forty-Seven, we will trace what life was like for an Egyptian under the oppressive rule of their Greek masters.

It is a long and fascinating history, but the study of Egypt should not end with this course. There will be suggestions of how to continue learning about Egypt—societies to join, events to attend, books to read. The adventure should not end here.

Lecture Twenty-Five
The End of Dynasty XVIII

Scope:

Here we will see what happens when a pharaoh dies leaving no heirs. The end of Dynasty XVIII is unusual—beginning with Tutankhamen, three successive kings of the Amarna Period died leaving no children. We will first examine the brief reign of Aye, Tutankhamen's successor, then the far longer reign of Horemheb, the last king of the dynasty.

Outline

I.   Aye (1325–1321 B.C.), who had followed Akhenaten to el Amarna, succeeded Tutankhamen as king at about the age of 60.

    A. He married Ankhesenamen, Tutankhamen's widow.

    B. He also appropriated Tutankhamen's tomb in the West Valley, a spur of the Valley of the Kings. Tutankhamen chose the West Valley because his grandfather, Amenhotep III, was buried there, and he wanted to distance himself from his heretic father, Akhenaten.

        1. Aye's tomb—and sarcophagus—is like Tutankhamen's, probably a nod to the latter's popularity.

        2. One wall has a painting of baboons as in Tutankhamen's tomb, probably made by the same artist.

        3. Ankhesenamen does not appear on the walls of Aye's tomb.

        4. Eventually his tomb, like so many others, was robbed.

II. His successor, Horemheb (1321–1293 B.C.), also childless, was a law-and-order pharaoh.

    A. He began his career as commander of the army under Amenhotep III, and his career probably floundered during the reign of Akhenaten.

    B. He was King's Deputy under Tutankhamen.

    C. He married Mutnedjemet, "Sweet Mother," perhaps Nefertiti's sister.

    D. Horemheb was a throwback to the centralizing tendency of the Egyptian past.

1. He counted his reign from the death of Amenhotep III, as though previous pharaohs never existed.
2. Thus, the heretical period spanning from Akhenaten to Aye didn't "exist"—he was rewriting history.
3. The names of Akhenaten, Tutankhamen, and Aye are simply missing from the kings lists. A minor king, Smenkare, also "disappears" from the record.
E. Many new policies were instituted during Horemheb's reign.
   1. Priests were taken into the army to cement military-state relations.
   2. He established two commanders of the army—one for the South and one for the North.

III. Horemheb also instituted many building projects for his own glory.
A. To build the ninth pylon—a huge gateway—at Karnak, he tore down Akhenaten's temples and reused the blocks as fill for the pylon. Ironically, he thus preserved Akhenaten's temples, though in altered form.
B. He usurped Tutankhamen's monuments. Everywhere he found Tutankhamen's name, he erased it and carved his own.
C. Tutankhamen had erected a "restoration stela" at Karnak. The stela says that all across Egypt, the statues of the gods had been melted down, weeds were growing in the temples, and the military was no longer respected—Akhenaten had allowed the country to collapse.
   1. What did Tutankhamen really think of criticizing his own father's reign?
   2. Horemheb, as soon as he became king, changed Tutankhamen's name on the stela to his own.
D. Tutankhamen, under advice from Aye, had also inscribed the Luxor Colonnade with scenes of the most sacred religious festival of Opet.
   1. Once a year, the sacred statues of the gods at Karnak were taken to nearby Luxor for a festival. Tutankhamen's inscription was a reminder of his respect for tradition.
   2. The names of Tutankhamen here, too, were replaced with Horemheb's. Everything of Tutankhamen's was wiped away.

E. Horemheb's Saqquara tomb shows his military career during Tutankhamen's reign, including the Syrian and Libyan campaigns. When he became king, however, he sent sculptors to alter his image at Saqquara so that it displayed the royal cobra on his forehead.

F. His real tomb in the Valley of the Kings (KV 57) was discovered by Theodore Davis in 1908. It contained wooden figures, symbols of royal power, similar to those found later in Tutankhamen's tomb.

G. Horemheb was the traditionalist, recalling Egypt to her great past. Such was the end of Dynasty XVIII. Because Horemheb had no heirs, the question again arose: Who would be the next king of Egypt?

Essential Reading:

Aidan Dodson, *Monarchs of the Nile*, pp. 113–118.

Supplementary Reading:

Peter A. Clayton, *Chronicle of the Pharaohs*, pp. 136–139.

Questions to Consider:

1. How did Horemheb's reign differ from Tutankhamen's?

2. What were the consequences of three consecutive pharaohs' not having children?

Lecture Twenty-Five—Transcript
The End of Dynasty XVIII

Welcome back. Last time, we took a little detour and talked about ancient Egyptian medicine. What I'd like to do today is bring us back to the XVIIIth Dynasty, and talk about how the dynasty ends. Now, one of the things that all Egyptologists talk about, when we talk about the end of the XVIIIth Dynasty, is the Amarna period.

You'll remember Akhenaten, the heretic pharaoh, moved the capital of Egypt north from Thebes 200 miles, to the middle of the desert, and established his capital, which he called Akhetaten: "the horizon of the Aten." But the modern local people there call it Tell el-Amarna. So we call this the Amarna period—the Amarna era. Amarna doesn't just refer to that town. It refers to the whole period, the art, everything involved, and it's all interconnected.

Now as you remember, Akhenaten tried to change the religion to monotheism, and it didn't work. When he died after 17 years of reign, everything went back to the old ways. Now he left as his successor his son Tutankhamen—young Tutankhamen—who had an advisor. Now he was only eight years old or so when he became king, so he's not calling the shots. He's not making the decisions. Somebody's making the decisions for him. And the best bet is that it's a man named Aye—A-Y-E—who becomes the vizier of Egypt. The equivalent of the Prime Minister, advising Tutankhamen, who had served under Akhnaten. Now, it's Aye, if you'll remember, who succeeds Tutankhamen by marrying the widow of Tutankhamen. Young Ankhesenamen. Aye is probably 60 years old when he succeeds Tutankhamen. All right. He's an older man by Egyptian standards, certainly, when he becomes the next king of Egypt. There are only two more pharaohs in the XVIIIth Dynasty—Aye and his successor, Horemheb. But it's all interconnected, as you'll see. This is all what we call the Amarna period. It's an unusual period for Egyptian history. What you'll see is we're going to have three kings in a row who don't leave any children. And that leads to turmoil. Who's going to become king?

The first of those three kings was Tutankhamen. If you'll remember, in his tomb two fetuses were found, probably miscarriages of Ankhesenamen. Both little girls. One was about eight months. One was about five months. But Tutankhamen did not leave a successor. But we know that Aye becomes king of Egypt. Now, remember, Aye started his career at Amarna. He was in with the pharaoh, Akhenaten. There are scenes of him, on his tomb wall, at Amarna, when he thought he was going to die there, at Amarna, of him and his wife. They're worshipping the Aten. So, he was kind of politically correct. He was worshipping the Aten, he was in with Akhnaten. But as soon as Akhenaten dies, it's Aye who says, let's forget this new religion. Let's go back to polytheism. Let's change all the ways. He has Tutankhaten change his name to Tutankhamen—remember, he wasn't born Tutankhamen. And then he says, we're going back to Thebes. So, he's the one who's calling the shots. And he's sort of guiding Tutankhamen, in the early days. But he becomes pharaoh.

He doesn't last long. As I say, by Egyptian standards, he's an old man. You know, the life expectancy, perhaps, from birth to death, in the ancient world, was about the 30s or so. He's 60-ish. He lasts only four years. He is king for approximately four years. Between three and four years and then dies. And is buried in his tomb. Now, what's important is where his tomb is. And you'll see it's politics that determines it, not looking for the best site, necessarily.

Aye is buried in the Western Valley. Now remember, the XVIIIth Dynasty, Pharaoh Tuthmosis I has the first tomb in the Valley of the Kings. And from him on, the XVIIIth Dynasty kings are buried in the Valley of the Kings, that main valley—until Amenhotep III. The great king, who has Egypt at its greatness, Amenhotep III, decided to put his tomb way off in the Western Valley, a spur of the Valley of the Kings. That's where Aye has his tomb. And you might wonder, why does he have his tomb off with Amenhotep III? Why? Why is it there? Well, it's a political reason. He didn't begin that tomb for himself. That tomb was begun for Tutankhamen. Not only did Aye take Tutankhamen's wife, he took his tomb. You see, as soon as you became king, you started building your tomb. And when Tutankhamen makes the journey from Amarna back to Thebes, he has to pick a site for his tomb. Now, Aye is his advisor. Tutankhamen is maybe, nine years old by now, perhaps. And Aye suggests, probably picks, I don't mean to say suggests. He probably tells him: the Western Valley. Why the Western Valley?

The answer is, it's a statement. And the statement is this: remember Tutankhamen's father was a heretic. He was viewed as trouble. He was the problem. Nobody liked Akhenaten in Thebes. So, when Tutankhamen is coming back, he's got to show, I'm a legitimate king. I've got royal blood in my veins. But he can't identify himself with his father, because he's the heretic. That's sort of bad. So Aye makes the decision, we'll bury you next to grandpa. Amenhotep III is his grandfather. The great traditional king. So Tutankhamen's tomb is selected as right next to his grandfather's. It's a statement saying, "I'm a traditional king. I'm not like my father." But Tutankhamen died suddenly. Perhaps murdered. His tomb wasn't finished. Barely started. So he was hastily buried in another tomb that was at least further along in construction, in the Valley of the Kings. So he's quickly buried in the Valley of the Kings. The main part, leaving Tutankhamen's original tomb empty. And that's where Aye is buried. He takes Tutankhamen's tomb. And his wife.

Aye's tomb interesting, by the way, for another reason. It is quite similar to Tutankhamen's. Quite similar. Almost as if he wants to identify himself with Tutankhamen. And I think there's a reason for that. Tutankhamen must have been a very popular king. Returning everything back to the good old days. All the temples are going to be open again. The gods are back. So Aye is saying, I was with him. For example, on one of the walls, in Tutankhamen's tomb, there's a scene of 12 baboons. These are the 12 baboons that guide the boat of the solar god through the sky. Aye has the exact same scene on his wall. And if I had to bet, I would say it's the same artist who painted it. If you look at it, it looks like the same hand. I've looked at it closely. I think it's probably the same artist. So Aye is saying, I'm establishment, too. I'm a good guy. He even has a sarcophagus like Tutankhamen's. So there are many, many similarities. Aye is trying to identify himself with Tutankhamen. The only thing he doesn't have on his wall is Ankhesenamen. She doesn't appear on the walls of Aye's tomb. We don't know why. Maybe she's dead by now. But she's not there. So Aye only reigns for four years and dies. His tomb was robbed, eventually. His name carved off the wall, as we've discussed.

Horemheb is the next pharaoh. Now remember what I said. That Horemheb didn't leave children either. We're going to have three kings in a row with no children. Tutankhamen—no children. Aye—no children. And now, we've got another pharaoh with no children—Horemheb.

What do we know about Horemheb? Well, the first is, he's a military man. A career military man. He started his career, probably, under

Amenhotep III. And when Akhenaten moved the capital and sort of let the military go, didn't support the military, Horemheb didn't go to the new capital. Horemheb stayed behind at Memphis. So he was probably pretty much languishing. As Akhenaten lets the military go downhill, Horemheb is just sort of hanging out, not doing much. So he wouldn't be a supporter of Akhenaten under any circumstances. And it's the old thing—it's sort of like the hawks and the doves, and Akhenaten is the dove. And Horemheb would, certainly, be the hawk, wanting strong military presence. So Horemheb began his career under Amenhotep III. Maybe, probably, languishes under Akhenaten. For about 17 years. Remember, Akhenaten rules for 17 years. But then Tutankhamen comes into power. That's when we see Horemheb really go up. His stock goes up.

He has the title of "King's Deputy" under Tutankhamen. It's an important, a very important position. And he's a military man, strong law and order. He marries a woman named Mutnedjemet. It's a great name, by the way. "Mut" is "mother." "Nedjemet" is "sweet." So, it's like, "sweet mamma," that's what her name means. Mutnedjemet. Some people think that she was the sister of Nefertiti. Nefertiti, the wife of Akhenaten. So some people think that he, Horemheb, is trying to show, well, I'm a little bit related to the royal family. I don't think she really was the sister. It's the same name. Nefertiti did have a sister named Mutnedjemet. But it doesn't mean that this is that Mutnedjemet; it's a common name. But he marries this woman, Mutnedjemet. And during his reign, when he becomes pharaoh, he's going to institute lots of new policies.

Now, think about it. He's a military man. He's what we would call a "law-and-order candidate." Straight arrow. Firm. There's a wonderful statue of him in the Metropolitan Museum of Art. It was carved when he was the king's deputy, when he was working under Tutankhamen. And it shows Horemheb as a scribe. Now, Horemheb, it's even possible, just possible that Horemheb was illiterate. He couldn't read and write, because most Egyptians couldn't. But it shows him as a scribe. It's a position everybody wanted to be kind of seen as. He's sitting cross-legged. He's got a papyrus roll on his lap. And along the base of the statue and on top of the scroll are hieroglyphs. And basically it says, you know, I'm the king's deputy. And it says, I'm a straight arrow, I'm a law-and-order candidate. I'll give you a little quote from the statue. It says—now, remember, he's an important official under Tutankhamen. It says, "I am the recorder of royal laws, who gives direction to the courtiers. Wise in speech. There's nothing I ignore. Without forgetting my charge." So, he's law-and-order; he sets things right. Interestingly, by the way, the inscription talks about the gods. Now, this is under Tutankhamen. It shows how quickly things are going back to normal. Horemheb is associating himself particularly with the god Toth—the god of writing, the god of law and order, keeping the records. So, things are going back to normal. And Horemheb is all for it.

So Horemheb had this career under Tutankhamen. And then he becomes the next pharaoh. Now, he does some really strange things. I mean, almost unique. One of the things he does, is, he acts as if all the subsequent pharaohs after Amenhotep III never existed. Now, what I mean by that, is this. Horemheb ruled for about 28 years. Roughly. If you look at the records that Horemheb's scribes kept towards the end of his reign, it says he ruled for 58 years. Now, what's going on? Horemheb is totally ignoring the reigns of actually four pharaohs—let me explain. He's pretending that this heresy period, anything connected with Amarna—when they tried to change the religion, when the military was allowed to go downhill—he is pretending that it never happened. He will wipe out the records of Akhenaten the heretic. Also, Tutankhamen. Because he was the son of the heretic. He'll even wipe out Aye's records. Because he was an advisor to Akhenaten. He will wipe out every trace of this heresy. And he will say, my reign comes right after Amenhotep III. So he's really adding, in a sense, 30 years to his reign. Because, if you figure out who ruled when, Akhenaten ruled for 17 years. Tutankhamen, for about 10. So, that's 27. And then, we've got Aye. Three. You've got about 30 years there, that he's just saying never happened. It's a "1984"-type thing; he's rewriting history. And if you look at the kings' lists, you know, the lists that all the pharaohs kept, you will never see Akhenaten, Tutankhamen, or Aye on those lists. There's even one other pharaoh that Horemheb wiped out. A mysterious pharaoh. We're really not sure who he was. We know his name: Smenkare. He ruled for only one year, as co-regent to Akhnaten. And we don't know who he was. Was he Akhenaten's brother? Was he Tutankhamen's brother? We just don't know. And some people think—remember I talked about Tomb 55? That tomb in the Valley of the Kings? Some people thought maybe that's the mummy of Tutankhamen. But it was a mix of things. It had a shrine for Queen Tiye. It had this, it had that. Some people think that may be the tomb of Smenkare. But Horemheb doesn't talk about him either. So there are really four kings who disappeared. So Horemheb is going to sort of wipe out all traces of the Amarna revolution. It's quite interesting.

Now, he has some new policies that he's going to institute. The first is, he wants priests to be integrated into the army. You know, this is like, the first military chaplains. This is the beginning of it. And the reason is that, I think, I mean, this is my suggestion, Horemheb saw that the priests were so powerful that they could actually force Akhenaten to get out of Thebes—you know, when he's trying to close down the temples and they're saying, wait a second. Akhenaten actually had to move out of Thebes, if you'll remember, to his new capital. Horemheb saw that. Horemheb knows priests are powerful. And why not integrate them into the military? Have them as allies? So he's thinking, he's not going to let what happened to Akhenaten happen to him.

Also, he's an army man. He knows the army very well. He has two commanders for the army. He knows the army is going to be big. It's a bureaucracy. And one person can't watch it all. So he has a commander for the north, and a commander for the south. Because remember also, communications were difficult. You didn't just pick up the telephone. You know, a couple of days. A boat going north. A boat going south. So, he's shaking things up.

Now, he also has building projects. Remember, every pharaoh wants to build. Wants to show that he's a great builder. And he goes to Karnak Temple, which is the greatest temple on earth, in Thebes. And he builds a pylon for himself. Now remember, a pylon is a huge gateway. And they're huge. They're like, 100 feet high. And the reason you build a pylon is that it gives you a large surface that you can write on to tell about how great you are. And they almost always have the same scenes. You always have the same scenes. The king is smiting his enemies. The king is making offerings to the gods. And he actually builds two pylons. Called the ninth and tenth pylons. All the pylons at Karnak are numbered. He builds the ninth and tenth pylons. But he does it in an interesting way. Remember, these are people. These are real people we're talking about. These are places that you can still walk today. Think about what had happened. Akhenaten had built his temples at Karnak. Then he moves to Thebes. Then he moves away from Thebes, to Amarna. Akhenaten's temples are at Karnak. And now Akhenaten dies. And everybody is going back to Thebes. And you still have these temples to this god the Aten, that nobody, really, particularly likes. A reminder of a bad time. Well, our man Horemheb fills his ninth pylon with the blocks of Akhenaten's temple. He takes down the temple. They must have been a kind of sore, open sore, reminding people of hard times. So, he takes all of these blocks. You know, like 40,000 of them. Takes them down. They're smaller blocks. They're not like pyramid blocks. They're about oh, I'd say, two and a half feet wide. You know, two men can lift one fairly easily. And he takes all these blocks, which are carved with scenes of Akhenaten worshipping the Aten. And he uses them as the fill inside his ninth pylon. He packs the pylon inside so he doesn't have to quarry stone. It's a cheap source of stone. You know, it's only a couple of hundred yards away. Now, there's a kind of curious irony to all of this. By taking down the temple and putting the blocks inside his pylon, he preserved Akhenaten's temple. He preserved it! And in the 1920s, when there was restoration work on Horemheb's pylon, and they had to take it down, they discovered all these blocks. And that's when they tried to reconstruct—on paper—Akhenaten's temples. By using the computer, as I was telling you. You photograph each block. And you try to say, well, we've got the head of a pharaoh. Where is a block that has the shoulders of the pharaoh? Maybe it matches. And that's how they reconstructed what Akhenaten's temple looked like. But it's because Horemheb tore it down.

Now, he does other things. He usurps all of Tutankhamen's monuments. Now, think about this. He was the king's deputy. Under Tutankhamen—that was his, really, heyday, almost. Until he became pharaoh, of course. But it doesn't matter. Every monument that Tutankhamen had been advised to erect, by Aye, probably, Horemheb takes Tutankhamen's name, carves it out and inserts his own. That's why it's so hard to find any information about Tutankhamen. Remember, I said he's the mystery king. He's the most famous king in history, but we don't know anything about him. Because they were erasing all traces of him. He was associated with this heresy time, the Amarna heresy. His father was the heretic pharaoh. So Horemheb comes in and erases all traces of Tutankhamen.

For example, Tutankhamen erected a stela, like all kings do. You know, the round-top stone, at Karnak temple. It's called the "Restoration Stela," because of what it says. Now, obviously, he's been advised, by Aye what to say. And what it says is, "When I became king, the temples were in disarray. There were weeds growing in them. All the statues of the gods had been melted down. The military was not respected. If it rode off, nobody attended." So he's really saying, Egypt had gone downhill under my father's reign—Akhenaten. So, Tutankhamen has this stela erected. It's called, "The Restoration Stela." because, in the end, he says, "I will restore it all. I have had new statues of the gods made. The temples are open again." So Aye was wisely advising him. You know, this is what the people want to hear. He erects this stela. But, you know, you do wonder—What does this kid think? I mean, he had grown up with his father, at Amarna. And now, somebody's saying, this is what we're going to say: Your father really did a bad job. You wonder what little Tutankhamen thought. But, anyway, the stela is erected.

Horemheb, as soon as he becomes king, puts his name on the stela. You won't find Tutankhamen's name on it. If you look very carefully—the stela is in the Egyptian Museum in Cairo. You go there, you can see it. It's off in a corner. Nobody ever looks at it. Nobody knows what it is. People walk by it. But if you look very carefully, where the king's name is, the cartouche, it'll say "Horemheb." But if you look very carefully, you'll see that it's carved deeper than all the other hieroglyphs. Horemheb came, carved out Tutankhamen's name, and then carved his name. So Horemheb is erasing all traces of Tutankhamen. All traces.

Also, there's one other monument that's very important for Tutankhamen, but you're not going to find Tutankhamen's name there. It's called the "Luxor Colonnade." When Tutankhamen's grandfather died, he left a monument unfinished. He had started a hall with tall columns. That's why it's called a colonnade. He had built it at Luxor Temple. But it's undecorated. And then Amenhotep III dies. When Akhenaten moves to Amarna, it's left undecorated. It's an unfinished monument—unfinished. When Tutankhamen moves back from Amarna to Thebes, Aye advises him: Finish this monument. Why? You're going to be associating yourself with grandpa—the establishment guy, that everybody loved. So, Tutankhamen's major monument during his 10 years of reign is restoring, completing, the Luxor colonnade. Now, how do you do it? How do you decorate it? What do you put on it? What he put on it were scenes of the "Opet Festival." It's the most sacred festival in

Egypt. He's a traditionalist. He's saying, look, I'm not really my dad's kid. I'm grandpa's grandson.

Now, this was a wonderful festival. The major three gods of Thebes during this time were Amun, "the Hidden One," Mut, his wife, and Khonsu, their ram-headed son. The trinity. Always triads for all the gods. These gods had statues at Karnak Temple. Now Karnak Temple is only about a mile and a half away from Luxor Temple. And once a year, during the festival of *Opet*, the statues of Amun, Mut and Khonsu, these sacred statues, would be placed in a little boat shrine and taken from Karnak to Luxor, where they would spend a fortnight or so. And Luxor was called the southern harim. And it would be a great festival. People could see the statues of the gods, there was drinking, there was eating. And the king paid for it all. It was a wonderful town feast. That's what Tutankhamen puts on Luxor colonnade. That's the decoration that he has. So that he's really saying to everybody, I'm traditional. It's back to the good old times. So he does that, which is a nice thing. And you know, Tutankhamen took part in this festival. There are scenes of Tutankhamen making offerings to the gods. But if you look very carefully, at Luxor Temple—you know I've been there a lot—you can't find Tutankhamen's name. They've all been erased. Where you have an image of Tutankhamen making offerings to the gods, the cartouche is a little deeper. And there's Horemheb's name. Horemheb came right in and just usurped the monument. So everything of Tutankhamen is going to be wiped away. That's why we hardly know about him. Because he was part of this Amarna heresy.

Now what about Horemheb's own monuments? Well, Horemheb has two tombs. Now, he only has one body. Why does he have two tombs? Because, first, when he was the king's deputy, when he was a commoner, he needed a tomb. So he built a tomb at Saqqara. Remember Saqqara, where the Step Pyramid is built? This was a place where people of the XVIIIth Dynasty—the nobility, people who are up and coming, not royalty, had tombs. There's a wonderful street of tombs. You can walk down and you can see. Oh, so-and-so, the treasurer, was here. The general was here. So-and-so was here. And Horemheb built a tomb for himself at Saqqara. Now, as a military commander, as the king's deputy, it's a pretty impressive tomb. Beautiful carvings. And you know what it shows? It shows Horemheb being rewarded for his good service by the pharaoh, who's probably Tutankhamen. He's being given gold collars. He's standing up. And he's got his arms up so the collars can be placed over his head. And people are coming and placing gold collars around Horemheb, as his reward for good service. Now remember, he's not going to be buried here, though, because he's going to become king. So he's going to have a tomb in the Valley of the Kings, where he will be buried. But it's kind of interesting. I mean, vanity is sort of an interesting thing. The tomb at Saqquara is not going to be used as the burial place for Horemheb. Because when he becomes king, he's going to want to be buried with all the big honchos in the Valley of the Kings.

What he does, though—I mean, the tomb is almost complete. It's decorated. It's got scenes of military exploits, all kinds of things. When he becomes king, he sends sculptors to the Saqquara tomb, to change it a little. Now, how are they going to change it? They're re-writing history. Horemheb the general is shown being rewarded with his collars of gold. And he tells the sculptors, wherever you see my picture, carve a little cobra on the forehead. Now the cobra is called, by Egyptologists, the *uraeus*. It's a technical term. It's simply Greek for "cobra." The Egyptians never used that word. *Uraeus,* it's a Greek word, used later. It means "cobra." The cobra was the sign of royalty, of the king. If you look, for example, at the famous gold mask of Tutankhamen, he's got a cobra coming out of the forehead. As a matter of fact, you know what's interesting. It almost became the symbol of Egypt. In sign language, international sign language for deaf people, the word for Egypt, you put up your finger like a cobra to your forehead. That's the word for Egypt. So it became a sort of symbol of Egypt. So, Horemheb says, well, you know, I really am king. He sends the sculptors up, and they carve the little cobras on the forehead wherever Horemheb's image appears. But, as I said, he's buried not at Saqquara. Not good enough for the king. He's buried in the Valley of the Kings. His tomb was found in 1908 by Theodore Davis. That wealthy American who was excavating in the Valley of the Kings and gave up, thinking he had found Tutankhamen's tomb. He found Horemheb's tomb. And I'll tell you something interesting about it. There are a lot of similarities between his tomb, or, at least, the things found in his tomb and Tutankhamen's.

It's a return to tradition. Tutankhamen's tomb has not been found yet. (1922 is when his tomb was discovered.) In 1908, they found the tomb of Horemheb. It had been robbed. A nice sarcophagus. Even some bones. Perhaps Horemheb's bones. They weren't examined carefully. So Horemheb's mummy may, well, bones, at least, may exist. But they also found wooden statues. Broken. Badly broken. But they had been gilded. And some had been painted black. And they were—from the fragments, you could tell what they were. There was once a statue of the king, standing on a panther, ready to harpoon. There were heads of panthers. These are kind of royal symbols of power. Things like that. In 1922, when Tutankhamen's tomb was found, statues just like that were found, but they were intact. So we could sort of reconstruct the statues that were in Horemheb's tomb from Tutankhamen's tomb.

Horemheb was the traditionalist, returning Egypt to great things. And what he had to do for official reasons, what he wanted to do, was erase all traces of the Amarna heresy. So he wiped out everything. Including Aye. So you've got no traces. No real official records of Akhenaten. That king Smenkare, Tutankhamen, and Aye. Horemheb says, it's Amenhotep III, and then it's me. In the tomb of one of Horemheb's nobles, are pictures of statues of the kings. He's got them lined up. And right next to Amenhotep III, Horemheb. So there was nobody in between. He had rewritten history.

And that's how the XVIIIth Dynasty ends. With the commoner, Horemheb, a military man, who probably takes over by military force—which is often how it's done. It ends with a military man as king. When he dies, [he] leaves no heirs. There are no children. And the question becomes, who will be the next king of Egypt? I'll see you next time.

Lecture Twenty-Six
Mummification—How We Know What We Know

Scope:

Mummification was a trade secret, and the Egyptians didn't leave records of how they did it; thus, detective work is needed. In this lecture, we learn about the four papyri that give Egyptologists clues about how the Egyptians mummified their dead.

Outline

I. Ask any curator what draws people into museums, and he or she will tell you, "mummies." For a long time, little was done to conserve mummies because they were considered dead people, not artifacts. In Egypt, mummification was the Big Secret. Why?

   A. There isn't a single papyrus that tells us how to mummify.

   B. The secrecy derives in part from the fact that the details were considered trade secrets.

   C. Two existing tombs show mummies in late stages of mummification.

II. The first of four papyri, the "Embalmers' Archive," describes the Men of Anubis, or the lives of embalmers. Anubis is the jackal-headed god named for animals that feed on decomposing flesh.

   A. Embalming duties were varied—embalming families, sealing tombs, and maintaining the tombs.

   B. An oath of allegiance had to be taken. The embalming families apportioned parts of the town between them.

III. The "Rhind Bilingual Papyri," discovered by lawyer Alexander Rhind (1860) in an intact Roman tomb, is another important source.

   A. The tomb had been plundered. Rhind found damaged mummies and tags with their names.

   B. In a Roman-period tomb he found the papyri next to a gilded mummy.

   C. We learn about rituals in the Rhind papyri, not surgical procedures.

      1. For 35 days the body rested in the "place of cleansing."

2. Seven openings of the head and 17 members of the body are described. These are magical numbers.
3. Seventeen rituals and 70 days to burial also indicate magical numbers.
D. The wrapping ritual included naming the bandages.
E. A husband and wife died within 46 days of each other, and the papyri give important details about them, including the cutting of hair as a sign of mourning.

IV. The "Ritual of Embalming" is another papyrus dealing with mummification.
A. Here again we learn ritual, not surgical, procedures.
B. First, there are a few days of mourning.
C. The body stays in natron for 35 days in a place of cleansing.
D. On the 46th day after death, bandaging takes place.
1. Horus, the falcon-headed god, came with ragged bandages, perhaps a sign of ritual belief that one took familiar (used) things to the next world.
2. Frankincense was placed in the head, myrrh in the body. They helped dehydrate the body and keep it from smelling.

V. Finally, Herodotus describes the mummification procedure in some detail.
A. He describes the mourning procedure.
B. He details the price ranges of different "models."
C. As for the cutting, first a red line was drawn on the abdomen to indicate the incision.
D. The brain was removed through the nose with an iron hook and the internal organs taken out with a "sharp Ethiopian stone."
E. The body was steeped in natron—a salt—for 70 days, although an earlier Egyptian account says 35.
F. The Egyptians don't give us the details we want on mummification. Only the mummies can do this, as we'll see in the next lecture.

Essential Reading:

Bob Brier, *Egyptian Mummies*.

Supplementary Reading:

Salima Ikram and Aidan Dodson, *The Mummy in Ancient Egypt.*

Questions to Consider:

1. Why were mummification techniques kept a secret?
2. How do we learn about mummies?

Lecture Twenty-Six—Transcript
Mummification—How We Know What We Know

Welcome back. I'm glad you're here again. You've been absorbing an awful lot of Egyptian history. Let's take a break. Let's just take a deep breath and review what we've absorbed so far. We started with prehistory—700,000 years of prehistoric times. We saw Egypt united under Narmer. We talked about the mythology of this period. We then went on to the pyramid age. The Old Kingdom, where we traced the development of pyramids from the Step Pyramid right up to through the Great Pyramid of Egypt. We saw Egypt decline—the First Intermediate Period. We saw it resurrect with the Middle Kingdom; the great pharaohs, pulling it all together. Then we saw it decline again with the Hyksos; two declines. And then we saw it rise to greatness, with the XVIIIth Dynasty. And we traced the XVIIIth Dynasty, with its great kings—Hatshepsut, Tuthmosis III. And we talked about Tutankhamen and Akhenaten, right down to the end of the XVIIIth Dynasty. It's a lot of history, you know. It's a lot. And I'm glad you're absorbing it, still here with me.

What I want to do today is take a little bit of a detour from the chronological approach—a side trip. And I want to talk about something that's very Egyptian. Very ancient Egyptian. Mummies, which is my specialty. There is something about mummies that is very special. Ask any museum curator. What draws people into museums are the mummies. People want to see a mummy. I've often thought about what's special about them. I think part of it is that when you're looking at a mummy, you're looking at a person. A recognizable person, staring back at you over 3,000 years. There's something different. It's not just a statue. It's very different from an artifact. And I'll tell you something about that. That has caused problems.

As you know, the Egyptian Museum, in Cairo, is the storehouse of all great Egyptian treasures, and they have plenty of mummies. And for a long time, the mummies were in terrible condition. And the reason they were in terrible condition is that nobody thought of them as artifacts that had to be restored. Had to be preserved. They were kind of like dead bodies—you don't touch them. So little was done for the mummies to keep them, to conserve them. And they really deteriorated considerably. Just because they were mummies. They were a separate category. But mummies are very special. And it's one of the things that people think of when you think of Egypt. You know, you mention a few things—it's pyramids and it's mummies. And mummies are what people want to see. So there's something about mummies. No question about it. And so I'd like to take a little bit of a detour. And in some detail we're going to go into mummies. We'll do a few lectures on just everything about mummies. And by the end, I'd like you to be sort of little mummy experts.

First of all, as I mentioned before, the ancient Egyptians never wrote down how to mummify a cadaver. They mummified people for 3,000 years, and there is not a single papyrus that tells us how to mummify a person. There are papyri that deal with medicine, as we've seen. There's certainly religious papyri. But there's nothing that tells us how to mummify a person. Why? Well, one reason is, I think it's a trade secret. Embalmers were a kind of guild. Almost like a union. And I think they wanted to keep it within the family. Often, embalmers were families. It was a family profession. And you know, it's the same today. Funeral homes are usually family professions. The son goes into the profession. Or the daughter goes in because the father was doing it. It's not the kind of thing when a kid goes to school and says 'oh, I think I'm going to be an embalmer,' if the family is not in it. So this is a similar thing. It was kept within families as kind of family secrets—trade secrets.

Now, today, I want to talk about what if they never wrote down how you mummify, what did they tell us about mummification? How do you figure out how to make a mummy? One source—it's not a great source—are the tomb walls. As you know, they painted almost every aspect of daily life on their tomb walls. So maybe you'll get a picture of somebody being mummified? Not quite. You'll get pictures of people working in the fields. You get people at banquets. Drinking. Getting drunk. You get fishing, they're hunting. Nobody's being mummified.

The closest thing are two tombs, in Thebes, that show a mummy in the last stages. He's being wrapped. And what's neat about it is, it gives you a little detail that you wouldn't catch otherwise. I think it's kind of neat. The painting shows a mummy with two embalmers working on it. And they're just doing the last stages of bandaging. They've got little thin strips of bandage and they're wrapping it around. But what's neat, the detail that I like, is the mummy isn't lying on a table. It's not on a table. It's on two blocks. And the reason is—anybody's who's worked with bodies knows—you work on bodies, you put them on blocks, so to speak. You elevate them off the table. Because if you have to get under it, when you're passing the bandage, you don't want to have to lift it off the table all the time. So you could just simply pass it beneath the mummy. So these guys are working on a mummy that's up on blocks. Kind of very much like if you jack up a car. So they didn't have to lift the body every time. So it's a nice detail. But that's all the tombs give us. That's about it, in terms of the mummification process.

Now we have some papyri that are relevant. They don't tell us about mummification, but they're relevant. And that's what I want to tell you about today. I want to tell you about a few of them. One is called "The Embalmers' Archive." They were found in the area that we call the Fayoum. It's southwest of Cairo. And it's a bunch of papyri that are the records—it's an archive. They're records of families of embalmers. And as you know, they're not going to tell us how they did it. But they tell us something about the life of an embalmer. The profession.

First of all, they were called "Men of Anubis." That was sort of the name of the embalmers. Now, why Anubis? Anubis is the jackal-headed god. And he's shown as a man with a jackal's head. Now the jackal was associated with the dead, because jackals' digestive systems are such that they prefer rotting meat. So they used to prowl cemeteries, looking for old bodies to eat. Because it's sort of predigested protein. So the jackal became the god of embalming, Anubis. And at mummifications there would be a priest who wore a mask of a jackal. A big, black jackal's mask. And he was sort of representing Anubis. So these embalmers in the embalmer's archive are called "Men of Anubis." There were also a couple of other titles. One guy was called "Sealer." The sealer. He was in charge of the tomb. The embalmers, apparently, also had broad responsibilities. They weren't just going to mummify the body. "Here's your body, ma'am, good-bye." No. They also [had] kind of like a side industry, I mean, and people do this in industry all the time. You start out with one specific thing, and then you think, how can we expand?

Well, the embalmers, eventually, became the people who were responsible for tomb maintenance. To maintain the tomb. Now what do I mean by tomb maintenance? Isn't it you just shut the door? The guy is buried, and that's it? You walk away? Not at all. In Egypt, which is a civilization that went on, as you now know, a long time, there were problems. Questions of ownership of tombs. For example, I mean, imagine this: Your grandfather is buried in a tomb. And your father oversees the tomb, he visits it. And maybe you visit it. But what about 500 years down the road? Is anybody going to visit that tomb? Maybe your family dies out. And then the question becomes, whose tomb is it? Perhaps at some point it's robbed. The tomb is vacant. Now whose tomb is it? It belonged to your family. Nobody's around to claim it. There were many, many cases in the courts, the law courts in ancient Egypt, about tomb ownership. Somebody said, no, no, my family owned that tomb. They said, no, it's a vacant tomb. We took it. And they were arguing. So the job of these "Sealers," the guys who were in charge of sealing a tomb and maintaining it, was to keep track of whose tomb was whose. Kind of like cemetery caretakers. Hopefully, the families would be around and watch over the tomb. So you were paid a fee for doing this. And you might be paid a fee to make sure that the inscriptions aren't falling off the wall, things like that. So embalmers did a variety of things.

Now from this archive, we also have an oath of allegiance that the embalmers took. There were two families that this archive is comprised of; two family records. And the deal was, the oath of allegiance is, basically, from one family to the other, saying, I'm not going to encroach on your territory. So in other words, they carved out part of the town. Anybody dies in this area, that's yours. Our area is over here. So you had territories that were sort of divided among these embalming families. But as I say, "The Embalmers' Archive," as we call it, doesn't tell us much about the process. And that's what we really want to know. How did they do it?

Well, there's a couple of other papyri that give a little more information. And one is called the "Rhind Bilingual Papyrus." Now as you remember, papyri are named after the people who discover them, or who own them. And Rhind was Alexander Rhind. He was a Scottish lawyer who went to Egypt in the 1860s. He fell in love with Egypt, and excavated in it. Now, in 1860, right at the beginning of Rhind's looking around, he discovered a tomb. He was in the Theban area. He was actually not far from the Valley of the Kings; not far. In a neighborhood called Gourneh, which is honeycombed with tombs. Not tombs of the kings—kings are buried in the Valley of the Kings. But tombs of fairly well-to-do people. And he found a tomb that was sealed in plaster. The door had been sealed, and it had a stamp on it. It was sealed during the reign of Amenhotep III—New Kingdom. Our man, Amenhotep III, of the XVIIIth Dynasty. So he thought he had found an intact, XVIIIth Dynasty tomb. He was disappointed when he opened the tomb. He broke down the seals. Opened the plaster, went in, and it was a tomb that had been robbed. Terribly robbed. And probably re-sealed during the time of Amenhotep III. What he found on the floor of the tomb were many mummies— damaged. Terribly damaged. And also, on the floor, were 14 of what we call "mummy tags." Now mummy tags are little pieces of wood. They're like maybe twice the size of a dog tag that men would wear around their necks in the army. In the military. In the old days. And they're wood. And these had the names of the various mummies on them. They were placed on the mummies in the embalmer's workshop. Now, think about an embalmer's workshop. It's like a funeral parlor. You've got lots of people. You're not the only person who's dead. You have several bodies you're working on at the same time. And especially after they're wrapped, how do you know who's who? How do you keep track? Sometimes you might write on the bandages who it is. But always, almost always, embalmers put a tag on the toe, on the foot, like you see in morgues. You know, in the movies. A little dog-tag type thing, with the mummy's name and address, so to speak. This belongs to this family. So you'd have the information. Rhind found 14 of these tags on the floor. So this is a nice source of mummy tags. More than we ever found in one place.

But the good news is, Rhind kept going. In the back of this tomb, he discovered an intact tomb that the robbers apparently had missed. And it went down deep into the ground. It was a tomb of the Roman period. Late—when the Romans were occupying Egypt. But it was intact. He found a stone sarcophagus, a nice wooden canopy around it. The lid was removed. And inside, there's a gilded mummy. Now, by gilded I mean the mummy had been sort of coated in gold. A little bit. On the face, especially. Gold was the metal of immortality. Now, the reason is that gold never tarnishes. Silver, as you know, you've got to polish it forever. But gold doesn't tarnish. So because gold doesn't change, the hope is that you'll associate the mummy with gold. The mummy will be unchanging. Untarnished. Undamaged. For eternity. As a matter of fact, in tombs, the burial chamber was often called "The Gold Room." So he's found this mummy. Rather nice mummy. Gilded. A kind of—made of leaves—kind of crown around the head.

But more important for us, on the left side of the mummy was a papyrus. This is one of the Rhind Bilingual Papyri—what I told you we were going to talk about at the beginning. First of all, let me say this. The papyrus is—it's a misnomer to call it "bilingual." It's not two languages. But in the early days they tended to do that. It's 1860. They just discovered it. They name it. It's bilingual. It has two scripts. It's the same text in *demotic*, the period of the language, or the script of the late period. And also *hieratic*, which is a cursive form of hieroglyphs. So it's Egyptian. That's the only language. But it's Egyptian in two different scripts. But the important thing about this papyrus is it tells not how to mummify, but it tells the details of wrapping and some of the rituals. This is a key source for us. A key source.

Now, what does it say? One of the things it says is that the mummy is left in the "place of cleansing" for 35 days. Now, "place of cleansing." It's interesting. We know that the mummy was at some time placed in a substance called "natron," to dehydrate it, for about that length of time. And it sounds like that's what the "place of cleansing" is. So we think that—how long was it placed in there? Thirty-five days. So the mummy is dehydrating. Perhaps for 35 days. It also tells us a little about the magical rituals that took place. And numbers were important in embalming. For example, it talks about the seven openings of the head. Well, it's got to be the eyes, ears, nostrils, mouth. Seven was a sacred number. There were also seven sacred oils that were used in preparing the mummy. And it also talks about; the 17 rituals that have to be performed on the body. And it even says there are 17 parts of the body. And you wonder. Seventeen parts of the body. And if you had to sit down and figure out parts of the body, you'd never come up with 17. But it was a magical number. They wanted to come up with 17. What are the parts? Let's see if I remember them. They're the seven openings of the head. They say there are four internal organs. There's lots more than that. But there were four sons of Horus. Horus had four sons, who protected the internal organs. And they usually talked about it as if there were just four internal organs. So they have seven openings in the head. We've got four internal organs. We've got two arms, two legs, and we've got a front and a back. That hopefully adds up to about 17. So they said there were 17 members of the body. And then it also said that the body had to be placed in the tomb after 70 days. So this papyrus is a good source of how long it took, what was going on. And we've got these numbers. Seven. Seventeen. Seventy. Seven is an important number. It also tells us that each bandage, as it's put on, has a name. There were magical names for the bandages. Because they were going to protect the arms. The hands. The fingers. So it was a big ritual, when you mummified. At least we know from this papyrus. It wasn't just, take out the internal organs. It was a big ritual that had to be done in a certain way.

Now, this "Rhind Bilingual Papyrus"—this is just one of them so far—also had drawings. There were drawings on the top of it. Little vignettes. And sometimes it showed the dead person lying on a funerary couch. Now a funerary couch is a special kind of bed. It had legs like the feet of animals. And sometimes it would have, at the head, where the headrest, headboard would be, a head of an animal. And it shows this: the deceased person lying on it, attended by the gods. Later, real ones would be found in Tutankhamen's tomb. But this was part of the ritual.

But this is only one of the papyri Rhind found in this tomb. The man's wife was also there. This was the burial of a man with his wife. Now, the man's wife died only 46 days after the husband. Didn't have much time to mourn. They both died in 9 B.C. It was during the reign of the emperor Augustus. And she had a papyrus also buried with her mummy, on the left side, almost a duplicate of the one for her husband. It's a curious thing. By the way, why bury them with the papyrus that tells you how to wrap a mummy? You wonder. And I wonder why they did this. But she was buried with one also. And there is a very interesting little touch about her papyrus. It says that she mourned her husband, but just for those 46 days. It's a little unclear. It could be 46. It could be 48, about that. So she mourned for her husband. And the word that they talk about when they say she mourned, it's an Egyptian word. But at the end there's a little ideogram. A picture. A determinative telling you what it means, it's a lock of hair. That's the symbol for mourning. Now, why? Because when a person died, mourning was an important part of the ritual. Very much like when we go to the funeral and that kind of thing. But what they would do is, the women of the house—and if it was an important person, the women of the village—would all tear their hair. They would pull out their hair. As a sign of, "oh, grief, how terrible it is." So hair became a sign of mourning. That's what the *Rape of the Lock* is about.

So anyway, the "Rhind Bilingual Papyri," these two papyri, one for a man, one for a woman, tell us something about how long the procedure took, what the wrapping was, about the rituals. But we really don't get the gory stuff. The nuts and bolts of embalming. We don't get that. But there's another papyrus that was found which is called the "Ritual Of Embalming." It's different from this "Rhind Bilingual Papyrus." The "Ritual Of Embalming," has a couple of really great details. First of all, it says the bandaging took place 46 days after death. Now that's interesting. That's a nice detail. If you combine everything we know, well, if it stayed in the natron or whatever, for 35 days. And it was a period of mourning, about three or four days, when the body wasn't handed over to the embalmers. So we're almost able to re-construct what happens to a body. A person dies. And then, you've got a period of mourning, that the family can get its grief out, see the body. It stays at home. It couldn't stay at home much longer, especially if it's hot. It starts to decay. It gets pretty, pretty, pretty smelly. But then it's brought to the embalmers on the west bank. And then put in natron for 35 days. And then, day 46 it's wrapped. Now, what happens for the rest of the days? Because we know it's supposed to be buried on the 70th day. So we've got a bunch of days.

The answer is, this must be a time for rituals. This must be when the priests say the prayers, where all kinds of rituals go on. So this helps us. There's a couple of other really great details in this papyrus. One I love—I think it's just so, almost, sweet. It has vignettes, again, little pictures that go with the text of this papyrus. And one of them shows the god Horus. The falcon-headed god. He's standing behind the funerary couch on which the deceased lies. And he's bringing the bandages that the deceased is going to be wrapped with. And the wonderful little detail is, that if you look at the bandages that Horus holds in his hands, you'll see they have ragged edges. That wasn't just that they happened to be that way. No. There was a ritual, I'm virtually certain, in which the bandages were made from the bed linens of the person who died. They were torn. Now remember, the Egyptians didn't have scissors, like we do. It's not easy to get an easy edge. It's not easy. But I think there was part of a ritual that you always were buried with some thing that you used in daily life. A little bit like a bride has some thing old, something borrowed, something new. This is something you went to the next world with, something familiar. So the family would probably tear some of the bed linens, give them to the embalmers to use. So even when the god Horus is coming with mummy bandages, they're ragged. The only bandages I've ever seen and I've looked at a lot of mummies.

The study of mummy bandages is something in itself. Textile people look at them. You can tell when the linen was woven, by how tight it is. You can tell whether the person was wealthy or poor by the quality of the linen. If you analyze what's in the linen, you can tell what resin was used to stick it. A lot can be done with just mummy bandages. And I've looked at a lot of mummy bandages. I've never seen mummy bandages that were finished on both ends. In other words, there's always at least one end that's ragged. Torn. You would think that if you were really wealthy, there might be an industry and just somebody weaving mummy bandages. So you could have new bandages for your mummy. But I think it was a ritual. I think that you weren't supposed to have new mummy bandages. The only example I can tell you of a mummy bandage that's finished on both edges, which means it was woven just to be. And it looks like an ace bandage. You know, kind of like Tutankhamen had in the little burial pit that was found near his tomb with the remains of his mummification equipment. There were bandages that were finished on both sides, which means that some weaver was hired to weave special bandages for the pharaoh. But that's the only example I've ever seen of finished on both sides. But this papyrus tells us a little bit about it. And it's kind of neat.

Now we still haven't gotten to the nuts and bolts. The "Ritual of Embalming" tells us one other thing that I think is important. It tells us what spices were used. What incenses were used for the mummy—frankincense and myrrh. And it says frankincense was placed in the head; I'm not sure exactly why. The brain was probably removed. Usually. So maybe it's put in through the nostrils. Maybe it helps the smell. But frankincense was for the head and myrrh was for the body. Often after they removed the internal organs they put spices inside—incense, so it wouldn't smell. It would help dehydrate and it wouldn't smell. So this tells us, also, about the incenses. So some details. But nothing surgical. Nothing clinical yet.

If you want to look for something clinical, the best place to go is our Greek tourist, Herodotus. Remember, he went to Egypt in 450 B.C., roughly. Saw everything. And wrote it all down. Now he was, of course, as anybody is who goes to Egypt, curious about mummies. Herodotus wanted to know. So he asked. Now, I am sure that Herodotus didn't see a mummification. Think about it. They're people like we are. If you were interested in how a person's embalmed, an embalmer isn't going to say, "come on over, I'll do one and you'll see it." It doesn't happen that way. But I think Herodotus was told a great deal. Now, remember, it's a trade secret. But not for Herodotus. He's a Greek. He's going back home. And he's going to write it down. So, Herodotus, 450 B.C., writes down how they actually did it. And he is one of our best sources. He's not an Egyptian writing how they did it. He's not an embalmer, a "Man of Anubis," writing how they did it. But at least he's telling us something about the surgical procedure.

Now he tells us a lot more, too. Really kind of a good guy, willing to tell it all. He tells us about the mourning procedure. He says when a person dies, the women tear their hair, tear their clothes, and throw sand on their heads. This, by the way, is indeed what women did in ancient Egypt. They did do that. We know; we have scenes on tomb walls of that. Also, he says, when they brought the mummy to the embalmer's shop, the embalmer would take out models of what you could get for your money. You know, here's the deluxe model. You know, they'd pull out a statue. Now, if you don't have that much money, we'll give you this one. And then we have the economy mummification. So there were three different price ranges, depending on what you could afford. Which is not unlike a funeral today. You know, the Egyptians were people just like us.

But Herodotus does tell us how they did it. At least, what he was told. Herodotus says that a man came and drew a red line on the abdomen. A red line. Now, this man is in a sense an anatomist, who was going to show the embalmers where to cut open the abdomen to remove the internal organs. And he says, then a man called the "slitter," a surgeon, in a sense, came. And with a "sharp Ethiopian stone"—Now, what is a "sharp Ethiopian stone?" It said with a "sharp Ethiopian stone," cut open the abdomen. He made the slit where the red line had been marked. A "sharp Ethiopian stone" is obsidian. A volcanic glass. Ethiopia just means "burnt face." It's the land of people who had burnt faces—black faces. So Ethiopian stone is a black stone—obsidian. So the man comes and cuts open the abdomen and then they remove the internal organs. Herodotus tells us that.

He also says they remove the brain with an iron hook through the nose. So that's apparently how they get rid of the brain. They know iron was in use in Herodotus's time—450 B.C. And they probably went in through the nasal passage with a hook and pulled out the brain a piece at a time. At least, that's what Herodotus is telling us. And then, he says, they placed the body in natron, this material that's going to dehydrate the body. And I'm going to talk about natron later.

But there's been a controversy because of the word Herodotus used for putting the body in natron. He uses a Greek word, which is the word that's used to preserve fish. So he's saying they preserved the mummy with natron, like fish. Now natron is basically a salt. And how do you preserve fish? Well, one way is to salt it dry. But you can also pickle it. You can also put it in brine. So for many years nobody was really sure. Did they put the mummies in a pickling solution for a while and then dry them out? Or did they put it in dry natron, salt it like fish, and then take it out? Nobody was really sure.

But Herodotus at least gives us basic details. Internal organs are removed. The brain is removed. The body is placed in natron for 70 days. He says 70 days. We have an earlier Egyptian account that says 35 days. We're going to have to reconcile that. And we will. But the point I want to make today is that the Egyptians certainly don't give us the details that we want about mummification. If we really want to figure out the details, we're going to have to look at the mummies themselves. And that's what we'll do next time. See you then.

Lecture Twenty-Seven
What Mummies Tell Us

Scope:

The primary source for figuring out how the Egyptians mummified their dead is the mummies themselves. In this lecture, we look at the detective work that enabled Egyptologists to reconstruct the ancient art of mummification. We will see the differences among mummies of the Old Kingdom, New Kingdom, and Late Period. By the end of this lecture, the student should be able to look at a mummy and tell how old it is.

Outline

I. The Egyptians mummified bodies for over 3,000 years. Old Kingdom mummies were intended more as statues than preserved bodies.

   A. Bandages were coated in plaster with facial details painted on the outside.

   B. The earliest effective attempt at mummification was Queen Hetepheres—"Wife of a king, mother of a king"—and is a mystery case.

   1. Her tomb was discovered this century near the Great Pyramid.

   2. Her internal organs were in her unplundered tomb. Natron, in solution, preserved them.

   3. Her sarcophagus was in the tomb. But when excavators opened the lid, they found no body.

   4. The excavator reasoned that Hetepheres was probably buried close to her husband, Sneferu, at Dahshur. Perhaps robbers destroyed the body, and the guardians told her son Khufu (Cheops) of the plunder, but that the body was safe—a lie to protect themselves. So Khufu had it reburied, not knowing that only the internal organs remained.

II. Mummies of commoners varied considerably.

   A. There were different price ranges for different services.

   B. Almost all bodies were eviscerated on the left side.

C. The brain was removed in higher-priced mummifications via the nasal passages.

D. Resin was poured in the skull to cauterize the area.

III. Royal mummies of the Deir el Bahri cache are a primary source of information.

    A. After wonderful jewelry began appearing on the international antiquities market in the 1870s, the hunt for a royal tomb began. Although arrested and tortured by the police, the grave robbers didn't at first reveal the location of the tomb they'd discovered. In 1880, they relented.

    B. Their find, soon revealed to the world, turned out to include a puzzling assortment of kings. The archaeologists found a passageway clogged with coffins from the New Kingdom:

        1. XVIIIth Dynasty kings included Tuthmosis I, II, and III.

        2. XIXth Dynasty kings included Seti I and Ramses II.

        3. The XXth Dynasty had an assortment of Ramses—including Ramses III.

        4. XXIst Dynasty royalty created the tomb.

    C. Several factors brought the burials to be together.

        1. The decline of Dynasty XX led to extensive tomb robberies.

        2. Priest-kings took control of Thebes and wanted to put away mummies in a safe place.

IV. Meanwhile, the royal mummies were quickly removed from the tomb.

    A. They were taken by steamer to Cairo at night.

    B. A great deal about Egyptian mummification was learned from these mummies.

        1. The brain was first removed in Dynasty XVIII.

        2. In Dynasty XXI, internal organs were replaced in the body. (False canopic jars and sons-of-Horus amulets were needed.) Through incisions, the skin was packed with an organic material for a more lifelike appearance.

    C. At the Egyptian Museum, the mummies were hastily unwrapped.

V. The Tomb of Amenhotep II (KV 35) provided the second royal cache.

A. In 1898, Victor Loret found the tomb of Amenhotep II. The mummy of the pharaoh with the bad teeth, Amenhotep III, was also there.

B. In fact, almost all Egyptians had bad teeth, because their bread was packed with sand from their grindstones.

Essential Reading:

Salima Ikram and Aidan Dodson, *The Mummy in Ancient Egypt*.

Supplementary Reading:

Bob Brier, *Egyptian Mummies*.

Questions to Consider:

1. What was the major difference between mummification in the Old Kingdom and mummification in the New Kingdom?

2. How did all the royal mummies found at Deir el Bahri come together?

Lecture Twenty-Seven—Transcript
What Mummies Tell Us

Welcome back. I'm glad the mummies didn't scare you away. We're going to do some more mummy business today. What I'd like to do is show you that the mummies themselves are perhaps the best way to figure out the process of mummification. Last time, we saw there were a few papyri that talked about mummification. But not really how to do it. They told us about wrapping, about the incense, about some of the rituals. And that the body had to be placed in the tomb after 70 days. But they really didn't give you the how-to. And I'd like to talk a little bit more about that today. And as I say, the best place to start is with mummies.

Now first, not all mummies are the same. You know, we tend to think of a mummy as a mummy is a mummy. But remember, the Egyptians were mummifying for 3,000 years. Certainly the process was going to change. They were going to get better at it, and maybe even worse at it sometimes, just like cars. Not all cars are the same. The "Model T" is different from a modern car. So they changed. And they got it better and maybe worse after a while. But not all mummies are the same.

Let's talk about mummies of the Old Kingdom. Now remember the Old Kingdom is the era of pyramid building. It's the era of Sneferu and Khufu. If you look at an Old Kingdom mummy, you get the feeling that they weren't really intending to preserve the body. They were really trying to make a statue, almost. If you look at Old Kingdom mummies of fairly wealthy people, very often what you've got is a layer of bandages that have been coated with plaster. And the features of the deceased are painted on the plaster, or sometimes carved into it. And what you're really making, almost, is a statue of the deceased with his body inside. But there isn't a great deal of preservation of the body going on. It's kind of—I think—almost in case the body is destroyed, you've still got the plaster coating. So the *ka*, the soul, will know where to go. So really, Old Kingdom bodies are not in very good shape. They weren't really dehydrating as we know it—removing the brain. None of that. It's more cosmetics. An outer shell that looks pretty good.

By the way, you know, the Egyptians aren't the only ones who mummified. And in Asia there are some mummies that are quite similar. Quite similar to Old Kingdom mummies. Meaning they're kind of good on the out side but not so good on the inside. There are some Vietnamese mummies of priests of the 16th century who are basically lacquered. They died, they were placed in a seated posture, and then lacquer was sort of painted over the bodies. And then gilded. So you've got them in temple shrines looking very much like statues. And they've been x-rayed. And inside you can see—inside the thing is just collapsed. The bones are all at the bottom; there's no skin holding it together. There's no tissue. And that's very much like the Old Kingdom mummies. They're kind of statues, but no real attempt at preserving well.

The earliest sort of good attempt at a mummy—an Old Kingdom mummy—there are a couple of Old Kingdom mummies that are pretty good—is Queen Hetepheres. Now Queen Hetepheres is an important woman in the Old Kingdom. She is the wife of my man Sneferu. Remember Sneferu, the one who showed Egypt how to build the pyramids. She's the wife of Sneferu. The mother of Khufu. The builder of the Great Pyramid. She's the wife of a king—King Sneferu—and the mother of Khufu. Real pyramid-building family. Her mummy is a great mystery story. I'll give you the facts, and you figure out what happened.

The tomb of Queen Hetepheres was discovered during this century by an American excavator from Boston, George Reisner. Great Egyptologist. It was found right next to the Great Pyramid at Giza, right next to her son's pyramid. It was found beneath the paving stone—tere's paving stones around the Great Pyramid. And the excavators found a sealed shaft, leading down to a small burial chamber. There was no question about it. This tomb was untouched for 4,500 years. An intact burial. Pretty impressive. Everybody was really thrilled. And they were going to do the opening of the burial chamber. And they had the important officials present of course, because this was an important tomb.

Now the first thing they found was a "canopic chest." Now let me explain about a canopic chest, what that means. As you now know from our man Herodotus, certainly at the time of mummification the internal organs were removed. These internal organs were eventually going to be placed in what we call "canopic jars." Four jars. And the jars are hollowed out, made of stone usually. And the lids of the jars are sometimes carved with the heads of four humans, four human heads. And sometimes they're carved with animal heads—three animal heads, one human. Sometimes it's the head of a human. Sometimes it's the head of a jackal. Sometimes it's the head of an ape. And sometimes it's the head of a falcon. These are the four sons of Horus. Horus, the falcon god, who avenges his father's death. The four sons of Horus are the guardians of the internal organs. They are supposed to guard the internal organs. So sometimes if you're a wealthy person you had canopic jars. And you had your little internal organs placed in them. Queen Hetepheres had a canopic chest. It was made out of alabaster—a big piece of alabaster, about the size of maybe a nightstand. And it was carved out into four sections. And in each of the four sections were Queen Hetepheres's internal organs. They had been put in a solution of natron—remember, that substance that's used to dehydrate the body. Natron is basically—I'll give you the chemistry and then I'll tell you what it really is. It's sodium carbonate, sodium bicarbonate and sodium chloride. It's basically baking powder and table salt; that's basically what it is. Well, there was a solution of that, and her internal organs were placed in it. So, fine, we have Queen Hetepheres's canopic chest. Her internal organs. And we know that she is our first mummy for sure who was eviscerated—who had the organs taken out during the Old Pyramid period. Fine so far.

Her sarcophagus is also in the tomb. Now as I said, various dignitaries were present for the opening of this sarcophagus, because this was a big deal. The tomb didn't have just a canopic chest and a sarcophagus. It had her furniture; beautiful, elegant furniture. She had jewelry. And remember Sneferu, her husband, sent expeditions to the turquoise mines in the Sinai. She had beautiful bracelets with inlaid butterflies made out of turquoise. Nice stuff, I mean elegant, elegant. And then there was her sarcophagus. Well various officials were lowered into the shaft—into the burial chamber. They had like a kind of a desk chair, a big chair, and they had a pulley system where they would crank the visitor down in the chair. They'd tie them in the chair, take them down. So they had this pretty crowded tomb. And it's kind of difficult to get around, to move. But they're going to remove the lid of the sarcophagus so all of the officials can be present at this great moment.

George Reisner, the excavator, is supervising. His artist was there—Joseph Lindon Smith—great artist. An archaeological artist who was recording what was going on. And they removed the lid. Sliding it slowly off. And Smith is the first one to look in. There's no Queen

Hetepheres. This is a sealed tomb. Nobody's been in it in 4,500 years. The internal organs of the queen are there. The furniture of the queen is there. Her bracelets are there. But the Queen isn't there. Smith looks inside. Now Reisner, the excavator, is a little bit off to the side, looks in, and he says, "George, it's a dud." The Prime Minister of Egypt says, "What's a dud?" (You know, it's a kind of colloquial term.) And then Reisner sees that there's no body in the sarcophagus. And he says to everybody assembled, "Gentlemen, Queen Hetepheres is not receiving today. But Mrs. Reisner has cookies up top." And that's what happened. The queen's body was missing.

Now what's going on here? Why is the queen's body missing when you have her internal organs? I will give you a theory. It is Reisner's theory. And I will preface it by saying Reisner read a lot of murder mysteries. That's what he loved to do. He loved, in his spare time, to read murder mysteries. And I think the murder mysteries influenced his suggestions to what happened. And by the way, Reisner gave his library—when he died—he willed all his books to the Widner Library at Harvard. And you can still get Reisner's murder mysteries. They're still there. And he annotates them—he says "good, pretty good, bad."

But anyway, Reisner suggests the following as a scenario. Queen Hetepheres, the mother of Khufu, wife of Sneferu, is buried first at Dahshur, where her husband had his pyramids. Remember, Sneferu built several pyramids. First the Meidum Pyramid which collapsed. Then he tried the Bent Pyramid, and that had difficulties. And finally he was buried in the Red Pyramid at Dahshur. Well his wife probably was buried close to her husband is what Reisner suggests. But after a while, her son is ruling. Khufu. Building his pyramid. Her tomb was robbed. Robbers got into her tomb at Dahshur. And perhaps, just perhaps, they destroyed the body. They were looking for jewelry. Often the bodies were destroyed because in the bandages are often magical amulets of gold, because gold is the metal of eternity. They destroyed the body but the internal organs remained. And other things remained, like the furniture.

Now the guards of the tomb are afraid to tell Khufu, "Your mother's body has been destroyed." I mean, she's lost her chance at immortality. They're afraid to tell the king, your mother's dead. Gone for eternity. Not just now. So what they do is, they reseal the sarcophagus. And they tell Khufu, "They broke into the tomb, but everything is okay. The sarcophagus was untouched. The internal organs are there. Every thing is fine." Because they're afraid to tell the king that the body is missing. So now Khufu decides, well, Dahshur isn't a safe place. I'm going to move my mother's body to where I'm being buried. I'm going to put her next to my pyramid, beneath the paving. So the body is moved. And Khufu feels his mother's body is intact, everything is fine. So it's buried just as if it was complete. And that may have been what happened. That was Reisner's suggestion as to what happened. It makes a nice kind of mystery story. It's possible. But the important thing for us is that Queen Hetepheres's body at least shows us, during the Old Kingdom a queen was eviscerated. The internal organs were taken out. So in the Old Kingdom they knew—if you really want to preserve a body, take out the internal organs.

Now as I said, there are all kinds of mummies. Good mummies. Bad mummies. They come in all kinds of shapes and sizes. And what you got depended, as Herodotus told us, on what you could afford. So the bodies of commoners, especially, varied considerably. But there's a certain sort of constants. As you know, the internal organs were taken out through a slit in the abdomen. Almost always, it's on the left side. A lot of people don't know—why the left side? Well, the answer is your body isn't perfectly symmetrical, you know. It's not. And the left side gives you better access to the descending colon. So I think it would be easier for the embalmers to get at it that way. So maybe that's why it's always on the left side. But almost all the mummies we see have been eviscerated on the left side. Also, in the better mummifications, we do see the brain removed through the nose, as Herodotus had said. So he was right there. And sometimes—remember, when we talked about Tutankhamen's skull—resin is poured inside the skull to kind of cauterize it. Hot molten resin is poured in. So there are certain things you look for in mummies to get an idea, what date was it? Was it a wealthy person? Was it this? Was it that? But you have to look at a lot of mummies.

And one of the greatest finds for students of mummies—people who specialize in mummies—was a cache of mummies called the Deir el Bahri mummy cache. Now these are royal mummies. And let me explain how this cache came about. Remember Deir el Bahri is a site on the West Bank of Thebes where Montuhotep built his temple, where Hatshepsut built her temple. They're next to each other. And the discovery of the Deir el Bahri cache took a lot of detective work.

In the late 1870's, fantastic royal jewelry began appearing on the Egyptian antiquities market. People were selling royal jewelry. Now where did it come from? Even Books of the Dead—beautiful papyri for kings and queens—were being sold. People figured that tomb robbers, modern tomb robbers, had found a royal tomb somewhere. In the Valley of the Kings, perhaps, they found a royal tomb. The head of the antiquities service, who was a Frenchman, Auguste Mariette came down. Trying to find out where the royal tomb was. Didn't find it. He died before they ever found it. But his successor, Gaston Maspero, another Frenchman—the French were running the antiquities service at this time—wanted to find that royal tomb.

Now one of his students, one of the students of Mariette, Charles Edwin Wilbour, an American—an American politician who sort of had to get out of town, and he left from Brooklyn. Left Brooklyn and he decided to devote his life to Egyptology. Fell in love with Egyptology. Became a scholar. Could translate. Spent most of his summers, you know, winters in Egypt. Summers writing up his notes. Translating inscriptions. A real scholar. Also a collector. Much of The Brooklyn Museum's wonderful collection of books was donated by Wilbour. Wilbour was in Egypt and Maspero wanted to use him to try to figure out who's finding what. And he bought some pieces on the antiquities market that belonged to kings. And Wilbour said you know, the Rassul family. Now they were a family of grave-robbers; went back many generations of grave-robbers. They lived in the town of Gourneh, right near the Valley of the Kings. And Wilbur thought, you know, it's got to be the Rassuls. He said, one of the Rassuls has a new white house. I bet it's built over the tomb. It wasn't. But indeed, the Rassuls had found the tomb. The Rassuls were questioned by the police. Now when I say "questioned," they were tortured. This was the 1870s, now it's almost 1880. They were tortured. One of the Rassul brothers limped for the rest of his life. But they didn't reveal where the tomb was. In 1880, I believe it was, the eldest of the Rassul brothers went to the police and said, I will show you where the tomb is. Apparently the brothers had made a deal or something. We're not sure. But he said, I will show you. Now the police are very sharp. They went straight to the Rassuls' house. Figuring they would have made one last trip to the tomb, gotten some goodies to sell in the future. And they did indeed find some things in the house. They did. But the Rassuls then took them to the tomb.

Now the tomb was more than anybody could have ever expected. The inspector who was sent down, his name is Émile Brugsch. Brugsch was sent down to see this tomb. He was led up a mountain pass near the Valley of the Kings. Not in the Valley of the Kings. It wasn't at all what anybody thought. He was led up a mountain path at Deir el Bahri, near Hatshepsut's temple. And there was a pit going down a shaft. And he was lowered down through this shaft. And then he went into a tomb, a passageway. But the passageway was almost clogged with coffins. Not one. Not two. But dozens of coffins. And as he walked through, there were also on the floor little servant statues that had been buried with these people. And there were things like boxes for the women's wigs. It was not just the coffins, but it was also some of the goods that went with them. And as he went by, there was another room and there were still more mummies. And coffins. Now he was a bit of a scholar. He wasn't a great scholar, Brugsch, but he could read the names on the coffins. And he couldn't understand what was happening. Because here were the mummies of the kings and queens of Egypt. Of different dynasties. For example, now you know some history by now—some of our Egyptian history. There was the mummy of Tuthmosis I, who had constructed the first tomb in the Valley of the Kings. There was the mummy of Tuthmosis III, the great warrior king. But there was also the mummy of Ramses the Great, who's from the next dynasty. There were also mummies of kings and queens of the XXIst Dynasty, still further into the future. How could these mummies spanning such a period of time all come together? Brugsch was really puzzled.

The answer, is that this convention of kings and queens came together because at one point in Egypt's history—and we'll get to that in detail—Egypt had slid again. It wasn't the power it used to be. And the Valley of the Kings was no longer guarded. So there was a rash of tomb robbings of the royal tombs. And a later king, when he took inventory—a king of the XXIst Dynasty—when he took inventory in the Valley of the Kings, he saw all these august ancestors had been defiled. He gathered them all together. And he wanted to put them in a safe place. A secret place, a hidden place. So he had this tomb constructed secretly. And that's how the mummies of Tuthmosis I, Tuthmosis III, Ramses II, Seti I, Pinedjem, Queen Henttowy—names we'll know, we'll be talking about in detail—

that's how they all came together in this tomb. And they lay there undisturbed until the 1870s when the Rassul brothers found it.

I'll tell you how I think they found it. These people, the tomb robbers, are very sharp. It rains in Egypt rarely. Especially in the south. Very rarely. But there is an occasional downpour. And that's when you look for tombs. You look to see where the water is running off, where it's disappearing into the ground. And probably they waited for a downpour and then they could see water disappearing. Another way you look, by the way, is at the ground—you look for stones that aren't like the stones of the area. You look for little fragments of pink granite—pink granite doesn't come from Luxor, you know, from Deir el Bahri, it comes from Aswan. So if you see little pieces of pink granite, you know, ah, somebody brought a sarcophagus in and it's been chipped. But there's some thing nearby. So two ways—you look for water running off, or you look for different stones. So the Rassuls, one way or the other, had found this cache of mummies.

Now Brugisch had the responsibility of removing these mummies. It was a great responsibility. Because the people of Gourneh, that village, had made their living by robbing tombs forever, and they would kind of view this as their heritage. And this was the gold mine of all gold mines. This was worth a fortune to all of them. And in a sense they were losing their heritage. So he had to move quickly. He was not able to take pictures. There were no diagrams drawn of where the mummies were. We don't know their exact placements. The earliest sort of description you get of this really is in the newspapers. *The Illustrated London News* had drawings of the mummies and it gives us an idea of what they looked like. But this was an amazing find. You had this elegant mummy of Seti I, looking just so beautiful. You had Ramses the Great. You had many of the great kings and queens of Egypt. And they were moved. Very quickly. He didn't want any robbery to go on. So a steamer—all these mummies were brought up, placed on a steamer, and they went to Cairo. They were going to be placed in the old Egyptian Museum which was then in Boulaq, a suburb of Cairo. Now it's interesting that as the mummies steamed along the Nile, people knew what was on that steamer. And the women of the villages gathered along the banks of the Nile and wailed. Just like a funeral, as they do today. And they wailed for their dead kings who were going by. It was rather eerie. Everybody who was there says, it's rather eerie.

But these mummies give us a really unique opportunity. Because you know what? For the first time we can see all of these royal mummifications. But even more important, these mummies provided the embalmers of ancient Egypt a chance to see how good their predecessors had done. Think about it. The king of the XXIst Dynasty is gathering bodies of the XVIIIth, XIXth, and XXth Dynasties. And they've been damaged; badly damaged. So he says to his embalmers, repair the bodies of the kings. Now for the first time ever, embalmers could see what a mummy looked like after 200 years. So they get an idea. And they weren't happy. They had really thought the mummification wasn't that good. So they did lots of new things.

Let me tell you what we learned from these mummies. First of all—remember I said the brain is removed through the nose. Well the first time the brain was ever removed seems to be in the XVIIIth Dynasty. That's when it starts, the removal of the brains. So that's something we know. And by the end of this lecture, you'll be able to hopefully look at a mummy, and you can figure out when it's from. If the brain is removed, you know it's after the XVIIIth Dynasty. If it looks like a statue rather than a well-preserved body you know it's Old Kingdom. There are many, many suggestions.

One of the things that happened though is when they looked and they saw that there were all these robberies, all these problems, they decided—in the XXIst Dynasty—that rather than take out the internal organs and place them in canopic jars—because when the robbers came in they knocked over the canopic jars, the organs were stepped on. Destroyed. It wasn't safe enough. In the XXIst Dynasty, they would dehydrate them and then put them back inside the body, inside that incision. So that in a sense the body would be intact. So that robbers, even if they did something, the internal organs would be inside. So now you don't need canopic jars anymore.

But you know, you still want those sons of Horus to protect you. So they did two things. In the XXIst Dynasty, they had little amulets in the shape of the sons of Horus. One is a little jackal, who was not Anubis. It's a different jackal. Called Duamutef. Another is in the shape of the ape. Another is the shape of a human. Another is in the shape of the falcon. Each organ has a little amulet with it to protect it. But the other thing they did is, they also made false canopic jars. They made jars that looked just like canopic jars, made out of limestone. Head of a falcon, head of a this, head of a that. But the jars' lids don't come off. It's all one solid piece. It's a kind of false jar. But the idea is, you'll have the sons of Horus to protect you. So for a while they put the organs back into the mummy.

But one other thing they did—I think it was because when they looked at the mummies, they weren't pleased with what they saw. They looked at the mummy, and it looked emaciated. It really didn't look like a person. A recognizable person. If you knew Ramses the Great, and you saw his mummy, you'd say, oh, there's Ramses's mummy. But it doesn't look like a living person. So the embalmers of the XXIst Dynasty started a new practice. They made incisions under the skin of their XXIst Dynasty kings, and they put a white material like … not fabric. I don't mean fabric. It's kind of a cheesy-like material; an organic substance under the skin and pushed it all the way in, literally fleshing out the skin. After the body is dehydrated, it looks pretty skeletal and cadaverous. Well they fleshed out the body. They made it look a little bit more lifelike. So that's a new development. If you find a mummy with incisions in the skin, often under the armpits, often they fleshed out the cheeks—you know it's after the XXIst Dynasty. So not every mummy's the same.

So these mummies were all taken to the old Egyptian Museum near Cairo. And some of them were quickly unwrapped. They didn't learn much. They didn't really know how to study mummies. They were unwrapped, and I feel bad about that. They should have been left as they were. But many, many were unwrapped.

But this wasn't the only royal mummy find. There's going to be one more. In 1898. The new head of the Antiquities Service, Victor Loret, a Frenchman, found the tomb of Amenhotep II. And in the tomb was a side room. And in that side room were other royal mummies. It had been bricked up with stone. They were great mummies. I mean important mummies. And one of them, one we know very well now, the mummy of Amenhotep III, the grandfather of Tutankhamen and the father of Akhenaten—that mummy was there. The mummy with the bad teeth. Because of that discovery, that's how I can tell you that he had bad teeth, and maybe couldn't rule at the end of his reign.

You know, one of the reasons the Egyptians had bad teeth was the bread. It was packed with sand. See, when you grind things on a grindstone, you always get a little bit of the grindstone in your bread.

And in a desert country, more sand. So as the Egyptians were eating their bread, it was grinding down their teeth. Like sandpaper. So almost all Egyptians, commoners and kings, had bad teeth. But this tomb, of Amenhotep II, gave us some more royal mummies.

And the best way we have of figuring out the process of embalming so far has been to actually look at the mummies. But there's one more way you can figure out how they embalmed. And that's by actually doing a mummification. And that's what I did a few years back. And I'll tell you about that next time. About when I took a human cadaver and mummified it in the ancient Egyptian style. See you then.

Lecture Twenty-Eight
Making a Modern Mummy

Scope:

In this lecture, the student sees how experimental Egyptology attempts to answer old questions. I describe my own research in which I mummified a human cadaver in the ancient Egyptian manner to determine just how the Egyptian embalmers did it. The purpose of the project was not to get a mummy but to answer questions in three specific areas: (1) How was natron used in mummification? (2) What surgical procedures were performed during mummification? (3) What tools were used by ancient embalmers?

Outline

I. We went to local sites to find such important substances as natron, frankincense, and myrrh. Natron was the essential ingredient in mummification, but there are questions about how it was used.

   A. Herodotus, because of an ambiguous term he used about preserving fish, started the debate about whether natron was used dry or wet.

   B. Natron, basically salt and baking soda, was more likely to have been used dry than in solution.
   1. No vats have ever been found for its use in solution.
   2. It is counter-intuitive to soak something you want dehydrated.

II. Tools of the embalmer were another puzzle.

   A. The Egyptians had used bronze knives, so we had to recreate some.

   B. The "necrotome," thought to be an embalmer's knife, was useless. We made bronze alloy blades—88 percent copper, 12 percent tin—just like the originals. *Kmt*, the ancient word for Egypt, is the root of our word *chemistry*.

   C. But "a sharp Ethiopian stone" (obsidian) proved to be the best knife of all.

D. Finally, "a hooked iron rod" of bronze was efficient for brain removal.

III. Surgical procedures were also replicated.

    A. The liver was removed by making a small incision with the obsidian. Obsidian blades are sharper than surgical steel.

    B. We removed the organs, even the liver. There is no Egyptian word for some organs, such as the pancreas, because the embalmers never saw it when removing the intestines.

    C. There were *four* canopic jars for internal organs—but what about other organs, such as the gall bladder and spleen?

    D. We left the heart inside and filled the cavity with a pocket of natron.

    E. Everyone thought the brain would have to be removed piece by piece with a "coat hanger." But the first embalmers must have rotated their tool, in effect whisking the brain, then turned the body over and drained the liquid.

    F. Embalmers probably worked outdoors because of the foul smells. We controlled humidity in our tent and covered the body with natron.

    G. We made an embalming board and left the body there. But for how long?

IV. Overall findings revealed the details of embalming.

    A. We left the body for 35 days. We found that the natron process—not the passage of time—gave the mummy its unique look. The body lost about half its weight, but there was still some moisture in it.

    B. We returned it to the "tomb" for a couple of months, and the moisture disappeared. It was so dry, in fact, we couldn't even cross the hands in the royal style. The 35-day injunction, mentioned earlier, referred to the period when the body was still flexible enough to manipulate.

    C. Our conclusion: A mummy looks like it does not because of the passage of 3,000 years but because of the procedure. Thirty-five days in natron, it turned out, was just the right time.

V. Future research will be done with the modern mummy.

    A. Our mummy is the only "ancient Egyptian mummy" whose method of preservation is known in detail. This is the "control mummy" for future experiments.

    B. Mummy DNA studies are now being conducted.

Essential Reading:

Bob Brier, *Egyptian Mummies*.

Supplementary Reading:

G. Elliot Smith and Warren R. Dawson, *Egyptian Mummies*.

Questions to Consider:

1. What surgical procedures were essential for mummification?
2. How was the body dehydrated during mummification?

Lecture Twenty-Eight—Transcript
Making a Modern Mummy

Hi. Welcome back. I'm glad you're back for mummies again. This will be our last lecture this time on mummies, I promise. But I want to tell you about my own research; a project I did a few years ago. And one that I think was important. Remember, we talked last time about how the mummies themselves give us clues about how mummification took place. The reason I did this project, the reason I actually took a human cadaver and mummified it, was to learn the details of mummification.

Let me tell you how it sort of came about. I was writing a book on Egyptian mummies. And the usual party line among Egyptologists is, we know all about mummification. They took out the brain through the nose. They removed the internal organs. They dehydrated with natron. We know all about it. But as I was writing the book and I tried to give a really detailed description of mummification, I kind of did a mental mummification. I realized there were loads of details we had no idea about. There were questions that had never been asked. For example, if you want to dehydrate the body, do you drain the blood first? Or okay, you put the body in natron—how much natron? Or, when you look at mummies, there are little incisions, very small incisions in the abdomen. The incision is only about two-and-a-half inches long. Can you really get a liver, which is the largest organ in the human body, out of an incision that small? So there were plenty of specific questions that had never been asked, that I really thought ought to be answered. And that's why I started the project.

Now let me emphasize something. We did the project. And I say "we" because I had plenty of help. We did the project not to get a mummy. We did the project to get knowledge. And it's knowledge about three specific areas. Let me mention the three areas, and as I explain to you the project, keep those three areas in mind. You'll see it always—everything we did relates to one of those three areas. One was, we wanted to know just about everything about how the natron was used. How was that substance, that baking powder, baking soda and salt used? We also wanted to know also about the surgical procedures. Exactly what were the surgical procedures? How do you remove a liver through an incision that small? How do you get a brain out through the nostrils? And then we wanted to know about the tools of the embalmer. These people were professionals. But what were the tools that they used? Nobody had ever found tools labeled, you know, embalmer's knife, embalmer's this. We weren't sure what the tools were. So these three areas: surgical procedures, tools, natron. That's what we were looking for.

Now in order to really learn how the ancients did it, we had to do it in the authentic way. We couldn't take any shortcuts. Couldn't do anything different. And when I say we, Ron Wade, my co-researcher in this project who is an anatomist—he's the Director of the State Anatomy Board at Maryland—he was the one who worked with me. And we worked very closely together on this. And we felt we had to do it just the way the ancient Egyptians did it. So for example, for the natron I went to the Wadi Natrun in Egypt—*wadi* means "riverbed" it's a place outside of Cairo—about 60 miles out, where the ancient Egyptians gathered their natron. Remember that for the natron Herodotus had said—he had used the words as if salting fish, or preserving fish when he talked about how they used the natron. So we weren't sure if it was dry or wet, and we were interested in seeing if we could preserve a mummy in one way or the other.

Our feeling was that it wasn't used in solution. Our feeling was that the natron was actually used as the powder, as it naturally occurs. And there are two reasons with this. One is—think about it, if the Egyptians really did mummify human cadavers in a solution of natron, there would have had to have been thousands of vats, large tubs in which these bodies were preserved. And we've never found such vats. So it's unlikely that they mummified all these bodies in a solution. Also, it's counter-intuitive. It doesn't make sense, if you're going to try to dehydrate a body, to stick it in a liquid. Not for the Egyptians. Especially since their idea of mummification came from the bodies that were naturally mummified in the dry sand. So our feeling was, they probably mummified in a dry natron. And that's how we were going to do it. So we got our natron just where the ancient Egyptians had gotten theirs. For our incense—frankincense and myrrh—I went to the spice bazaars in Cairo and bought it from the spice merchants. And they got it from exactly where the ancient Egyptians would have gotten it—from Yemen, from the Sudan. So we had our natron, we had our frankincense and myrrh.

Now we needed our tools. Now as I said, no one's ever found nicely labeled embalmer's tools in any excavation. And we looked at tools to see what would be the best. What would seem like the best bet for an embalmer's tool? There's even an article that had been written by a previous scholar about one tool which he said was almost certainly used for mummification. It's a knife which has a notch in the blade. Now the reason—and he even called it the "necrotome," the "death knife"—the reason he thought it was used by embalmers is, imagine if you're an embalmer. You're working in a slit that's only about two-and-a-half inches in the in the abdomen. You can only get one hand in probably. And how do you cut things easily with a knife? Well if it has a notch maybe you can kind of loop it around. And then pull it. Yank it. And that's how you cut something with the notch. We made a knife just like the ones that had been found with that notch. It was useless; didn't work at all for mummification. So we're quite sure he was wrong about the "necrotome"—the "death knife."

But we had to use other things also. So we made knives, replicas of knives that were found in excavations. Now we made them just like the Egyptian knives. The Egyptians had bronze knives. Bronze is made of tin and copper. And we made our knives just like the Egyptians. Eighty-eight percent copper, 12 percent tin. And we also discovered, by the way, that you can't cast a sharp bronze knife like that. It won't take a sharp edge. What you've got to do is beat it. So it had to be folded and beaten, folded and beaten into shape. And that's how we made our bronze knives.

Bronze, by the way, must have been a little bit of a miracle for the Egyptians. The reason I say that is, what you do with bronze is, you take two soft metals. Copper is soft, and tin is soft. You put them together and you get a hard metal. How does that work? I mean it must have been a little bit like a magic trick. It's because of the molecular structure, of course. The reason tin is soft and copper is soft is the molecules are long in it. And it slides. You can pull it. They literally slide. So when you combine them you get a latticework. It's much tougher. The Egyptians apparently knew how to do this, though. They could combine these two.

You know that's why, by the way, we have the name chemistry today. Chemistry comes from the ancient Egyptian word for Egypt, *kmt*. Kmt. It was K-M-T. Kmt. That was what the Egyptians called Egypt. And they were skilled at things like metalworking. Making ceramics. The kinds of things we think about as being chemistry today. And the Arabs called it "al-Kemi." The sort of "skill of

Egypt." And from "alchemy" we got our "chemistry." So really, because the Egyptians could do things like this, we have the word chemistry.

Now we had to find someone who could do this kind of metalwork. And we found a silversmith. A third-generation silversmith, who could beat on knives from copper and tin making the bronze. So we had replicas of ancient Egyptian tools. Also, if you'll remember, Herodotus said that the "slitter" makes the incision with a "sharp Ethiopian stone"—obsidian. We found somebody to flake obsidian for us. So we had obsidian blades also that we could use. And really what was most useful, we had a simple flake. A chunk of obsidian flaked off—nothing fancy. But we would use that too. Now what about Herodotus saying a hooked iron rod was used to take out the brain? We found an instrument in an excavation and we made a replica of it. It looks a little bit like a coat hanger with a kind of hook at the end, a long thin thing. We made ours out of bronze. Because that's probably what they really used. But we had ancient tools to work with. Now the question was, would it work? Could we do it? So we began.

Now, when we started to make the incision in the abdomen—we did it the same way Herodotus said, by the way. Made a nice little red line, marked where we were going to cut, and then I took a bronze knife. Didn't work. It was just too dull. It really didn't work.

Most of us had thought that the reason Herodotus said a "sharp Ethiopian stone" was for ritual purposes. That maybe from the old days they used to use stones. But surely they had bronze knives. Why not use a real knife? The answer is, the bronze knives don't cut that well. But then when I took the "sharp Ethiopian stone"—the obsidian—the abdominal cavity opened up almost immediately. One gentle swipe through, I was down to the level of the adipose, the fatty tissues. And then another one and I was right into the abdominal cavity. It was as sharp as any surgeon's scalpel I had ever used. And I will tell you that today, modern times, right now, surgeons are going back to using obsidian scalpels. They are better than surgical steel. They are sharper; thinner edge and do less damage when you're making the incision. So the Egyptians knew what they were doing with their "sharp Ethiopian stones."

So we opened the abdominal cavity. And then we started removing internal organs. Now another thing that was of interest to us was, in what order did the organs come out? It'd be interesting to know. So first one out was the spleen. We took out the spleen. The big question was the liver of course. We really didn't know if it was going to come out of an incision two-and-a-half inches long. The liver is the largest organ in the body. And a human liver is quite large. It fills up both hands. If you cup your hands together, the liver will more than fill up your two hands. So we didn't really know if it would come out. We eventually got the liver out intact—not easily, by the way. We had to make the incision a little bit longer, about another half-inch. Kind of like an episiotomy when somebody's giving birth. Just make the incision a little bit longer. And finally the liver came out. The liver is made up of two lobes. It's not a single chunk, so to speak, it's two lobes. And one comes out and then the other one slides behind it. So we did get the liver out. This also, by the way, answered a question I had wondered about in mummification.

In the Metropolitan Museum of Art, in their exhibits, I had seen on display a liver from a mummification. But it wasn't really a whole liver. It was half a liver. And I sort of wondered why. And I think the answer is, sometimes they may have had to cut the liver in half. But we'll talk about that a little bit later. So the liver came out. We did figure out you could get a liver out of a small incision.

Now another interesting thing that we found was, you know in going back through various medical papyri, we found the Egyptian words for the different parts of the body. But for example, for some internal organs there is no word. Like pancreas. Now why isn't there a word for pancreas? They supposedly knew anatomy, or some anatomy. Well the answer came to me sort of as a shock. I hadn't been thinking about this. With my colleague Ron Wade, we were taking out internal organs, and we had taken out the intestines. And you know, you have 22 feet of intestines in you. It's quite a bit. And we tied them off. And we take out the intestines. We take out the stomach. And as we're going along, I said to Ron, "Ron, where's the pancreas?" And I said I hadn't seen it. And Ron said, "Oh, it came out with the mesentery. It came out with the intestines." You don't see it. It's kind of a mess when it comes out. It's a mass. It just came out. And I think that's what happened with the Egyptians. They just didn't really notice it that much when it came out with everything else.

So anyway, we took out the internal organs. And then we wondered –why are there only four canopic jars? The four sons of Horus— that's nice. But you certainly have more than four internal organs. The canopic jars were supposedly for the stomach, liver, intestines, lungs. What about other organs? Like the gall bladder? The pancreas? The spleen? Well, I think they just weren't important to the Egyptians. They may not have known the function. They may not have seen some of them. So I wonder what happened to them. Did they just get thrown out? Perhaps—it could be. But we were learning by doing. It was a kind of experimental archaeology.

Now we had other questions. We proceeded right along in Egyptian ways. For example, after we had evacuated the abdominal cavity, we left the heart inside. Just like the Egyptians did. Then we filled the empty abdominal cavity with little packets of natron. We had seen mummies that had little packets of natron inside. And that was to absorb the moisture from the inside out.

But I think the most surprising thing in these surgical procedures, in trying to learn about the surgical procedures, perhaps the most surprising was how the brain was removed. It didn't come out the way everybody thought. There had been some suggestions by Egyptologists, by physicians, about how the Egyptians removed the brain. Because we know it came out through the nose. Because we had x-rays. We can see the nose has been a little damaged. There's a bone behind the nose, the ethmoid bone, which was broken. And here's how everybody thought the brain came out. Imagine the cadaver lying on its back. It's supine. The nose is towards the ceiling. And now you take your long coat hanger-like instrument, put it through the nasal passage. You break through the ethmoid bone which is a little bone behind the eyes. It's thin. You can go through it. And now your little coat hanger-like instrument is inside the cranium, in the brain. And you pull it out. And it takes with it a little piece of brain. You keep repeating this process, many times if necessary. Pulling the brain out piece by piece. Everybody thought the brain came out that way. We tried it. It doesn't work. The brain is too—it's not viscous enough. It's not solid enough. Practically nothing adheres to that little coat hanger-like instrument when you pull the brain out. They couldn't have possibly gotten the brain out that way.

So we did some talking. "How do you think, Ron? What do you think?" And we finally figured out that what they must have done is put the coat hanger-like instrument into the brain and rotated it, using it almost like a whisk in a kitchen. Breaking down the brain. Then they invert the cadaver so the brain runs out in its liquid state. And that's what we did. That's how we removed the brain, by breaking it down.

And remember the Egyptians didn't know you thought with your brain. They believed you thought with your heart, because it's your heart that gets excited and beats quickly, not your brain. So we figured that's how they did it. Now the question is this—once they've gotten the brain out, how do you know you've gotten it all out? You have to get it all out, because you don't want the body to decay. And the brain will putrefy, because it's moist. And bacteria will work on anything that's moist. Well, we figured—I mean, we could have done an x-ray. But that would have been cheating. Because certainly the Egyptians didn't do an x-ray. What we figured they must have done, was taken linen. Thin strips of linen—and we did this—and force it back into the cranium with that instrument. And when you pull out the linen, it's going to come out red with blood. Some dural matter, some brain material, will be on it. Well put some more linen in. and we kept repeating that until the linen came out clean. Then we knew we had gotten all of the brain out. So the surgical procedures were now pretty much complete. The brain had been removed. We learned how they did that. Abdominal work had been done. Learned how they did that. Now we had to dehydrate the body.

So we tried to re-create what an Egyptian tomb might have been like in terms of temperature and humidity. We created a little tent. Now one of Anubis'—one of his names, remember—Anubis was the jackal-headed god of embalming. One of Anubis's names is "He who is in his tent." Because embalmers probably worked out of doors, because of the smells. And another name for Anubis is "He who is upon his hill." So Anubis worked high on a hill, in a tent, so the smells would go away. So we had set up a kind of tent indoors. But a kind of tent where we controlled temperature and humidity. We had the temperature at about 105 degrees. Hot. We kept the humidity fairly low, around 22 or so, 23. And we put our cadaver, our eviscerated cadaver, in this room, and we covered it with natron—dry natron.

One of the things we learned was how much natron it takes for a human body—600 pounds. That's a lot of natron. It took 600 pounds. So we covered it in natron. We put it on a board, an embalmer's board. One embalmer's board had been found in an excavation, and we made an exact duplicate of it. A wooden board. Interestingly, across the wooden board—it was a plank—were some things that looked like railroad ties. Other boards the size of railroad ties, but spaced out, about nine inches between them. We wondered why.

And then when we put the mummy, our cadaver, on the board we figured out why. When your heart stops beating, the only thing determining fluids is gravity. It goes to the bottom. And naturally you need most of your natron on the bottom of the body because that's where the fluids are going to settle. So these railroad tie type things allowed you to keep a lot of natron under the body. You know to fill it in with natron. Then you put the body on top of it. And then you pile natron on top of the body. So we put our body on this embalming board, in our tent, so to speak. One-hundred-and-five degrees, 22, 23 percent humidity, and we left it there.

Now the question is how long to leave it? Well, we had a couple of different suggestions. One, remember in the Rhind Papyrus, it said 35 days in the "place of cleansing." But Herodotus said 70 days in natron. Which was true. We figured we'd leave it for 35 days and see what happened. We think, and we're pretty sure we're right, Herodotus really was confused. It's 70 days for mourning. We knew that you had to put the body in the tomb after 70 days. So we left it for 35 days in the natron and we didn't look at it. And we were pretty good. We were wondering what would happen We didn't know if it would work. Would we get a rotting cadaver, or would we have something like a mummy? And that was another interesting question we wanted to answer. I'm sure you've never thought about it—but think about it now. When you go to the museum and you see a mummy, why does that mummy look like it does? Is it the result of the mummification process? Or is it because it's 3,000 years old now? Do you need 3,000 years to have something look like that, or did it really look like a mummy as soon as it came out of the embalmer's shop? Nobody knew. Because nobody had ever seen a mummy coming right out of the embalmer's shop.

So that's basically one of the things we were going to learn. Our mummy was going to come right out of the embalmer's shop. So we left it for 35 days. We thought we were going to be okay. I'll tell you why we thought we were going to be okay. With the human body, when it starts to decompose when baric bacteria work on it, you can smell it. It's a very strong smell. And we were working inside a medical building, and people didn't smell it. So we thought it was working, but we weren't sure.

After 35 days, we went in to look at our mummy. Now when we started to remove the natron we found that it was caked. It had almost become like cement. It was really caked. But we started to remove it. Chipping it away a little bit, brushing some away. And the first thing that came out of the natron was the hand. We could see the hand. And it looked just like an ancient Egyptian mummy's hands. So we now knew we had a mummy. And the reason the mummy looks as it does is because of not the 3,000 years, but the process itself.

So we had our mummy. And it was looking very much like an ancient Egyptian mummy, very much. Interesting is the weight loss. The mummy had lost approximately half its weight in the 35 days. Now part of it is the evisceration. We're taking out organs. We're taking out the brain. But most of that loss is water. Remember, you're mostly water. So if you're dehydrating you're going to get a pretty light thing. So a little bit more than half its weight was gone now. We took out our mummy to examine it. Now the first thing we discovered, it wasn't bone dry. There was still some moisture in the body, mainly in the larger muscle groups at the bottom. Like the gluteus maximus, the butt. Also the thigh muscles, the quadriceps, were still moist. You could still feel a little bit of moisture. The hands, the feet, they were really dry like an ancient mummy's. But there was still some moisture. And we wondered, what should we do? Should we wrap our mummy? Its final wrapping. Or should we put it back in natron? What to do? We weren't sure.

We decided we would learn more if we put it back in the tent, in its tomblike setting, without any natron. Just as if after 35 days it had been, so to speak, wrapped, and put back in the tomb. Will it decompose with no natron now? Or has enough moisture been taken out so that it'll remain without decomposing? So we put it back in the tomb for a couple of months, just left it there. And when we came back, it was fine. Dehydrated much more. Had lost more weight. It was now down to about 45 pounds. And we had our mummy.

Now it was time to wrap it. And we wanted to wrap it in a grand Egyptian style. As you now know, not all mummies are the same. We were doing a top-of-the-line mummy. We were doing a royal mummy. And we wanted to wrap it the same way royal mummies were wrapped in the XVIIIth Dynasty, with the hands crossed on the chest. And that's when we got our next surprise. And this may be the most important thing we learned from this experiment—we couldn't cross the hands. The mummy now was so dry it was brittle and inflexible. We couldn't cross the hands. So we wound up wrapping it with its hands at its sides.

But the point I want to make is this. The Egyptians in their papyri said 35 days. There's a reason for the 35 days. After 35 days, our mummy still had a little flexibility. It had a little bit of moisture. We could have crossed the arms, we could have done whatever we wanted. That's why they say, leave it in the natron for 35 days. After 35 days, you can still manipulate the body and wrap it in any position you want. Then you can put it back in the tomb. It'll dehydrate. Won't decay. And you're going to be okay.

So we figured out pretty much almost exactly how the ancient Egyptians mummified. Their goal wasn't as everybody had thought, get rid of every drop of moisture. Because moisture of course is the enemy of the body. This is why you know you can have dried foods forever. You know, you get your cereal with a little bit of dried blueberry in the cereal. I mean that's a mummy of a blueberry in a sense. It's dry, so there will be no bacteria working on it at all.

So the Egyptians didn't try for complete dehydration. They wanted maximal dehydration, so you could still have it flexible and wrap it, and then put it in the tomb and you'll be okay. I mean, it's remarkable what they figured out. But our idea was to replicate it in the exact way the Egyptians did it. It was kind of really experimental archaeology.

Now remember in the beginning, I said that we were looking for information in three areas. One was how the natron was used. And we showed that you could really use dry natron. How much. How it was used. That worked fine. We wanted to learn about the surgical procedures. We did indeed figure out how you can remove the brain through the nose. It wasn't the way people thought. You can get the liver out through a small incision. About three inches for a large liver. And we even learned about the tools—that sharp Ethiopian stone that Herodotus had mentioned was the best possible tool to use. It wasn't just because it was a ritual that had been done in ancient times. It was because this was the thing to use. It gave you a nice clean cut. Quick. Opens up the abdominal cavity. So we learned really quite a bit about the three things we wanted to learn about. But the experiment's not over.

The mummy, in a sense, is an ongoing project. We hope it'll be used literally for centuries to come. We get requests [from] around the world for samples of tissue. For x-rays of our mummy. And let me explain why. Our mummy is, in a sense, the only ancient Egyptian mummy, but it's of course not ancient Egyptian. But it's just like an ancient Egyptian mummy. It's the only ancient Egyptian mummy for whom we know exactly what was done. We know everything done to our mummy. Every procedure. We even put amulets inside, everything. And we of course have now x-rayed our mummy, CAT-scanned it. We know exactly what our mummy looks like. Now if somebody finds a mummy, an ancient mummy, and is wondering what was the procedure used on this mummy, in a sense our mummy is the comparison one—the control. You could x-ray that mummy, compare it with our x-rays, and see—"Ah, different from this one. They didn't do that. Or different from this." So in a sense, our mummy is a standard against which the real ancient Egyptian mummies can be checked.

Also, we periodically check our mummy to see, how is it holding up? It's now about—oh, it must be five years since we did this mummy project. And the mummy has been at room temperature. I mean if we did it right, it doesn't need refrigeration. Our mummy has been at room temperature for about five years. No signs of deterioration. It's even been on exhibit once in a museum. It traveled once. But we view it basically as a research tool. So we can now look at our mummy and say, this is what a mummy would look like after five years in a tomb. This is what a mummy would look like after 10 years in a tomb. This is what it looked like after 20 years. And maybe for centuries on. We'll see what happened to a mummy as it was left in the tomb. But that's not all.

For example, other uses of our mummy. DNA studies. You've all heard that DNA in mummies is a hot topic. That is will we be able to use DNA in telling relationships? Can we tell for example if Tutankhamen is related to Akhenaten, if we have the two mummies? Can we tell if this mummy suffered from this? Or what. DNA is an important study tool. And paleopathologists, people who study disease in the ancient world, are very eager to use DNA in mummies.

But let me emphasize, it hasn't been that successful. We haven't really been able to replicate ancient DNA very well. We haven't been able to work with it well, and we don't know why. One reason is perhaps the 3,000 years. Maybe after 3,000 years, DNA degrades. But another possibility is perhaps because of the mummification process itself. Perhaps when you mummify it destroys the DNA Well, our mummy's the control again. Our mummy isn't 3,000 years old, but it has been mummified. We are now trying to work with our mummy's DNA We have sent samples to laboratories around the world. And they are now trying to reconstruct the DNA of our mummy. If they're successful, then we will know that it's the 3,000 years that degrades the DNA in ancient Egyptian mummies. If they're not successful, we'll know it's the mummification process. So it's an ongoing process.

We're working with the mummy all the time. But the reason we did it was to figure out primarily how the Egyptians mummified— surgical procedures, tools, and the use of natron. Next time, it's back to business as usual, and ancient Egyptian history. See you then.

Lecture Twenty-Nine
Dynasty XIX Begins

Scope:

The end of Dynasty XVIII presented a unique and difficult situation. The last three pharaohs (Tutankhamen, Aye, and Horemheb) died without children, leaving the question of who would succeed them unclear. Egypt now desperately needed stability, and the first pharaoh of the XIXth Dynasty may have been selected not for his ability but because of his heirs. Here we will see a new dynasty seek to establish itself.

Outline

I. Ramses I (1293–1291 B.C.) ruled only briefly but established a dynasty.

    A. A commoner, the vizier and friend of Horemheb, his father was a general named Seti. Ramses had a son and grandson, so succession would be clear.

    B. His wife, Sitre, was the first buried in the Valley of the Queens.

II. His son, Seti I (1291–1278 B.C.), was the first great king of the dynasty.

    A. Seti means "follower of Seth." A vizier and general like his father, Seti started his own tradition.

    B. He took the title of "repeater of births."

    C. He married Tuya and had three children.
        1. One son died young.
        2. His daughter, Tia, lived to adulthood.
        3. The second son, Ramses, would become Ramses the Great.

    D. Seti I went on several military campaigns to reestablish Egypt.
        1. In Syria, he captured forts and returned with captives.
        2. He led a Libyan campaign in the west.

E. Seti built some of the most beautiful monuments in Egypt.

    1. He began the famous Hypostyle ("supports a ceiling") Hall at Karnak. The columns are so massive that 100 men can stand on the top of one.

    2. His temple at Abydos was the first major project after Amarna. An Egyptian temple, off-limits to commoners, was in fact, a hive of activity. The priests, who began as stand-ins for the pharaohs, were a professional caste who didn't have to be believers. Some of their positions were hereditary.

    3. The temple at Abydos has a great kings list. You won't see Akhenaten, Tutankhamen, Aye, or Hatshepsut included in the cartouches—it's as if they never existed.

    4. The temple contains seven sanctuaries (Re-Horakhty, Amun-Re, Osiris, Isis, Horus, Ptah, and Seti himself.) The Hall of Ancients honors Seti's ancestors.

III. Found at Abydos, the Osireion, a unique building, is also perhaps Seti's.

  A. The Osireion is 30 feet below ground level, and its huge blocks of granite are not typical of the period.

  B. The blocks are surrounded by an artificial moat that would have been filled with water.

  C. The building is called the Osireion because it was said to be the place where Osiris was buried after Isis reassembled him. (Another version of the myth says that his head was buried there.)

  D. There are two theories about the construction of the building.

    1. Most Egyptologists believe that Seti built it. Religious texts discovered in the tunnel leading to the monument are inscribed with his name. (Others suggest that Seti left his sarcophagus there while waiting for burial in the Valley of the Kings.)

    2. My own theory is that the Osireion is much *earlier* than that. The temple at Abydos doesn't follow the usual building plan, shaped as it is like an L instead of on a single axis.

    3. It may be that they discovered this monument while building the temple above, then turned left to avoid it. Seti simply took credit for the earlier work by making inscriptions. The size of the stones suggests a much older date of construction.

4. The nature of the repair work done on one block also suggests how Seti might have sought to get credit for work not actually done during his reign.

E. Seti died and was buried in the Valley of the Kings. His tomb ceiling is a beautiful astronomical design; his sarcophagus is made of translucent alabaster.

F. Seti had prepared his son—Ramses the Great—to carry on in his tradition.

Essential Reading:

Peter A. Clayton, *Chronicle of the Pharaohs*, pp. 140–145.

Supplementary Reading:

Aidan Dodson, *Monarchs of the Nile*, Chapter XI.

Questions to Consider:

1. Why was Ramses I, an old man, selected as pharaoh?
2. Why did Seti I build a temple at Abydos?

Lecture Twenty-Nine—Transcript
Dynasty XIX Begins

Hi. Glad you're back after all the mummies. I promise no more mummies for a while. What I'd like to do is bring us back to the chronological picture again, trying to proceed through 3,000 years of recorded Egyptian history. When we last left off our chronological history, we had the end of the XVIIIth Dynasty. Now let's recap a little bit. We had Akhenaten, the heretic pharaoh, try to change the three basic pivot points of Egyptian society. You know, he tried to change the role of the pharaoh, the military, and religion. After 17 years it was a failed experiment. His son Tutankhamen, being advised by a senior advisor, Aye—A–Y–E—goes back to the old religion. Moves the capital back to Thebes, and life goes on as normal. After Tutankhamen, we saw the old vizier Aye marry Tutankhamen's widow, Ankhesenamen. He's an old man, Aye. Only reigns for four years and then he dies. He's succeeded by Horemheb, a military man. Now this is not an unusual thing, even today. That when there's a weakness in the government, the military steps in and takes over. That's where the power is. That's where the stability is. So Horemheb, a military man, really seizes power and becomes king of Egypt. But as we also saw, we had an unusual circumstance. We had three kings of Egypt in a row with no children. Tutankhamen, no successor. Aye, no children. No successor. Horemheb, no children, no successor, and Egypt saw that this was a bad thing. So the next dynasty, Dynasty XIX, is going to make sure this doesn't happen again, and that's why they choose as the next king of Egypt, Ramses I.

So let's start with Ramses I. First of all, he's a commoner. He has no royal blood. Because nobody has royal blood anymore. Horemheb was a commoner. Ramses I is a commoner. He was the vizier of Egypt under Horemheb. So he's a friend of Horemheb, and Ramses I's father was a general. So he's a military man of sorts. So what we've got really is somebody who is a friend of Horemheb. The vizier who knows how to run the government. Military connections. Becomes king of Egypt. He's an old man, though. He's not going to last long. But I think the reason they pick him is not just that he's the vizier and knows how to run the country. Not just that he's militarily connected. Remember, Egypt had been thrown in to turmoil because the previous three kings didn't have a successor. Ramses I is picked as king of Egypt because he's got a son and a grandson. So at least for two generations we know there's going to be a succession and royal blood can start. So Ramses is king of Egypt. It doesn't last for long, as I say. Three years or so.

His wife by the way—there's a nice innovation during his reign. His wife, a lady named Sitre, is the first queen. She's queen of Egypt. She's the wife of Ramses I. This is not Ramses the Great by the way. It's Ramses I. You'll see. She's buried in the Valley of the Queens. This is a new innovation just as Tuthmosis I was the first pharaoh to be buried in the Valley of the Kings. There is now going to be a separate burial place for the queens of Egypt and she is the first inhabitant of the Valley of the Queens. But as I said, Ramses dies after only three years. We can't say much about his reign. But his son is a great king, the first great king of this dynasty. Seti I. Now he probably had served as vizier, just like his father. So he knew how to run a country. He's a curious case and let me say why. His name. His name is a little bit of a problem. Just a little. Seti. Seti. Sounds like the god Seth. It is. Seti means "eye of Seth." Meaning, I'm a follower of Seth. Now it's not quite a usual name. Not very common. There were people who had the name Seti. Seti I's grandfather had the name Seti. There are people who had the name Seti. But it is a little unusual—and remember these had been turbulent times. We had had a heretic king. Lots of turmoil. So Seti wants to show that he's going to be a traditional king, and as an extra name he has a name that means "renaissance." We've seen that once before. He's going to say, it's a renaissance. We're coming back. It's going to be good. And he marries a woman Tuya and they have children. The thing to remember for right now, he has a son that dies young. He has a daughter named Tia who will live to be an adult, and another son who's going to be Ramses the Great. This is the father of Ramses the Great—Seti I.

Anyway, Seti knows what to do. He goes to battle, just like the XVIIIth Dynasty had. He marches to Syria and he conquers a town that's very important in Syria. Kadesh. It's a town that had been controlled by Hittites. Now the Hittites are the ones from Turkey. They controlled it somewhat. But he takes control of—Kadesh. Kadesh is an interesting site, by the way. It's on a hill. It's one of these towns that's been built up over thousands of years. It's mounds. But he goes to Syria and he returns with captives, and he has battle scenes on his temple walls and shows himself as a warrior.

He knows what to do. But he's a builder. Loves to build. Builds some of the most important temples in Egypt. And today I want to tell you not just about what Seti builds, but what an Egyptian temple was like. What it was like to be inside one of these things.

The first thing he does is he builds at Karnak Temple. Now Karnak—remember we've mentioned it several times is on the eastern bank of Thebes, and was becoming the largest temple in the world. Karnak is not to be viewed as a temple. View it as a temple complex—temple next to temple next to temple, over 100 acres. A huge sprawling temple complex. A very important place. It's where the god Amun lived. There were different precincts even, it was so large. There was a precinct for Amun. There was a precinct for his wife Mut. There was a precinct for their son Khonsu. There was a sacred lake. A place where the bark shrine could be put on the water. It was a beautiful place, and pharaoh after pharaoh, to gain favor with the gods, had built his own temple. It doesn't make sense as a whole complex. You walk and you go left. You go right. Temple after temple after temple. And Seti is going to build there. He builds the Hypostyle Hall—the famous Hypostyle Hall.

Now, the word "hypostyle." It's an architectural term. All it means is, it supports a ceiling—it has a roof. This is the place where you have these massive columns. The columns are literally so massive that 100 men can stand on the top of one. That's how big they are around. A hundred men can stand on the top of a column. Seti builds this Hypostyle Hall and it must have been a beautiful place. You know, when you see it today, when the tourists see it today, the color is gone. But it was once brightly painted and you had papyrus painted on these columns, looking like they were almost growing out of the ground. And you had Seti's cartouche. It was a beautiful place. So he builds at Karnak Temple.

Now something about temple life and the priests who inhabited these temples. First, any Egyptian temple was basically off-limits to the commoner. It wasn't, as I said once before, like a church, where everybody is supposed to go, they're happy if you show up. They're thrilled if you show up on Sunday—no. This was a place where the gods lived. You didn't do your worshipping there everyday. You didn't do it once a week. Maybe you went there on a festival day, and you were allowed in to the open courtyard at best. Egyptian temples were generally built like a New York City railroad flat.

Straight, on one axis. Usually there were three parts to a temple. And Karnak as I say, is temple after temple.

Usually there are three parts to an Egyptian temple. First, you would always go through a pylon, anyway, the big gate where the king could put the great deeds that he had done. You go through the pylon, and then you're in the open courtyard, the first part of the temple. Open to the sky. Large open area. This is where, if it was a festival day, you might be permitted in—where they would bring out the statue of the god to the open courtyard, and then maybe you'd get a glimpse of it as the priests carried it.

Next, you enter into an enclosed courtyard. It's roofed over and it's getting dark. It's getting more mysterious, and then the third chamber—the holy of holies. This is where the cult statue was kept. It's not just a statue of the god. It's The God. Now these statues were usually bronze. Sometimes gold. If they were bronze, they were gilded and they were kept in a little shrine with doors that opened and closed, and only the priests—the high priests—were allowed into this holy of holies where the god lived. Now the god had to be fed. Clothed. Perfumed. And that was the job of one class of priests called the stolists. As in a stole, wearing a stole around your neck, around your shoulders. These were the stolists, who were in charge of the god's clothes. In the morning—there were rituals twice a day. In the morning, you would go in to the holy of holies if you were the priest. Open the doors, say the prayers, place some food before the god. Put cosmetics perhaps on the eyes, perfumes. And then the god would be ready for the daily activities. And you would do this several times a day. So this was a place which the living god inhabited.

Now in addition to these three rooms, there were some changes. Some alterations of this. But almost always around any large temple was an enclosure wall, and between the temple area and the enclosure wall was often where priests actually lived. Some of them lived there. But more important, there were temple workshops. It was a hive of activity. For example, priests only wore white linen. That was the garment of a priest, pure white linen. Remember by the way the Egyptians didn't have cotton. No cotton in ancient Egypt. It's linen which is made from the flax plant. So the priests wore white linen robes. Or a high priest could wear a leopard skin. The workshops are where they wove the linen. There were workshops all around. There were places that made garments for the priests. So it was a busy place.

Now the priests themselves. We have to understand, you know, when Seti I is going to build his temple at Karnak. We have to understand the mentality of what's going on, what he's going to try to do. Priests in ancient Egypt were not people who had a higher calling. They were not people who were dedicated to the god in a religious sense. No. They were people who were doing a job. They were professionals. And this probably comes from the earliest days of Egyptian civilization, when the pharaoh was the high priest of everything, and during the year the pharaoh would have to conduct all the rituals. He would perform all the rituals. He would go up and down on a boat on the Nile and stop at temples, and he would perform the various ceremonies that made sure that divine order rested in Egypt. At some point, obviously, the culture grew too big for the pharaoh to go everywhere. He couldn't do it. That's the beginning of the priesthood of Egypt. He needed a stand-in, or several stand-ins to go up and down the Nile and do the ceremonies, the rituals. So the priests begin originally as stand-ins for the pharaoh. They don't have to have any great calling or connection with the god. The pharaoh is the only one with the connection, who's really connected. These stand-ins are going to go up and down and act. They're going to be like actors. Theatricals were going to be performed. So the priests really don't have to have conviction. And this remained the *status quo* in Egypt for thousands of years. Priests did not have to have a feeling of a higher calling. So these were guys who were doing a job.

This is why, by the way—and it surprises people when they read this—many of the important positions of a priest, like a high priest of a certain temple, many of the important positions were hereditary. You had it; your son would get it. It was a good job. It didn't matter that he was an alcoholic. It didn't matter that he caroused with women. Didn't matter. He could still show up at the right time, say the right words and the business with the gods would have been conducted. So priests are not to be viewed as holy men. Don't think when every time you hear, "Oh he was a priest. He must have been a holy man." No way. So the priests were people. Just like other commoners, just like the laymen. But they knew the words to say.

So when Seti builds at Karnak this Hypostyle Hall, it's a bustling place. Temples all over the place and priests fighting with each other. The priests often vied with each other to say, "My god is better than your god." So there was a lot of competition. And if you were a really good priest, you could make a lot of money. Because the temples had land and the land was given to the priests. So you had plenty of chance to rise if you were a priest. So our man Seti builds at Karnak. A good place to build, showing "I'm establishment." But he also builds a temple at Abydos, in the south. Now remember, Abydos was the sacred place where Osiris was buried. This was the most holy of all cities in Egypt. Every Egyptian wanted to be buried at Abydos. Of course they couldn't. So if you weren't buried at Abydos, you would send a little statue or something to be buried there.

So Seti, when he decides to build his big temple at Abydos, is making a political statement. He's saying, "I'm mainline. It's back to the good old times. It's no more Akhenaten. Forget him. We're going back to traditional gods." Now he builds a beautiful temple at Abydos. Beautiful. It is in many ways the most beautiful temple in Egypt. And the reason, I think, is that remember during the reign of Akhenaten, our heretic pharaoh, the artists were given free reign. They weren't sort of hindered by tradition and you got some beautiful work during that period. Those artists were still alive. Those artists who had been allowed to give free reign to their creativity were alive, and they are probably the guys who do the paintings at Seti's Abydos temple. So you still have artists who had been given creative freedom ,but now they're going to apply it to traditional scenes. So he builds a beautiful temple at Abydos. Spectacular.

Now one of the interesting features of the temple—there's plenty of interesting features about this temple—is the kings' list. Remember, pharaohs were always very proud of their heritage. They loved to list: I'm the 112th king; and here's 111; and here's 110. Tracing back their lineage. There's a great kings' list at Abydos, in the "Hall of the Ancients." It traces the kings from Narmer to Seti I. It's rather beautiful, by the way. It's a long hall, and all you have are cartouches of the kings. "The Hall of Records," it's called. And there you see Seti I. He's about to read the names of his ancestors. Once a year, you would read the names of the ancestors so they would all have food and drink in the next world and in front of him is a little kid. A prince who's helping him. That prince is going to be Ramses the Great.

But if you look carefully if you read the names in the cartouches on the kings' list you'll see plenty. You won't see Akhenaten. You won't see Tutankhamen. You won't see Aye. You won't see them. They didn't exist. It's as if they never existed. You know who you also won't see? Hatshepsut. She's missing too. Because Egypt just couldn't allow it to be said that we had a woman who ruled as king. Seti has this lovely lovely kings' list. I mean it's beautiful. Highly polished. Quite something. But that's not all that's at Abydos. There's plenty at Abydos. He also builds chapels within his temple at Abydos. It's really quite an interesting place, and there are plenty of gods in the back. Let me tell you about the chapels. There are sanctuaries to Re-Horakhty who was Horakhty—"Horus of the horizon." He's a composite god. It's Re the sun god, and Horus of the horizon. There's a chapel for him. There's one for Amun-Re. The composite—Amun the hidden one, and Re. There's one for Horus, Isis, Osiris, Ptah, and there's one more for Seti himself. He is sitting there with the gods. Just like them.

So Seti is going to be quite a king. He builds the Hypostyle Hall at Karnak. He builds the temple at Abydos. He beats up on the Syrians—a great king. Great king. But behind his temple is one of the strangest monuments in all of Egypt. And nobody to this day is sure of what's going on with it. Let me describe it. There are two theories about this monument. But let me describe the monument first. I'll give you the two theories, and then you can decide which theory sounds most reasonable.

First, the monument is behind Seti's temple. But it's 30 feet beneath the ground level. In other words, if you were to walk right out of Seti's temple and keep running, you'd fall 30 feet. So it's well beneath the ground level. That's the first curious thing about this monument. Next, it's built out of huge stones. Huge blocks of granite. What we call monolithic. They are not typical of the XIXth Dynasty. Not typical of this period. They are monumental. Next, the blocks seem to be on a man-made island, and are surrounded by water. It looks like a very ruined temple surrounded by a moat, and indeed it is a moat. It's an artificial moat that was supplied by water from the Nile by underground pipes. So it's an intentional surrounding of the temple by water. It's called the "Osireion" because many people believe that it was intended as a kind of sacrificial or almost reverential burial of the god Osiris.

Remember according to the myth Osiris was hacked into many pieces by his evil brother Seth. Then Isis re-assembled Osiris, breathes life into him. Speaks the magical words and he becomes whole again. Now many people say there are different versions of the myth. One version says that Osiris was finally buried at Abydos—the entire body. So we have this Osireion as a kind of false burial. It's a physical burial for a mythological character. Osiris was buried here, and that's the purpose of this monument. To commemorate the burial of Osiris on holy ground at Abydos.

Another version of the myth, by the way, says that Osiris's head was buried at Abydos and that could also account for this monument. One of the names of Osiris is "He who sleeps in the water." "He who sleeps in the water." Because remember, part of him was thrown in to the waters of the Nile. So it makes some sense to think about a strange burial place at Abydos the sacred city, surrounded by water. So these were some of the stranger aspects of this monument.

But I haven't gotten to the theories yet about what it was used for really. Or who built it. The first theory, which I think most Egyptologists subscribe to—most—it was built by Seti I. It's right behind his temple at Abydos. That's one reason. But there's a better reason for thinking that Seti built it. The monument was originally reached by a covered tunnel, and on the walls of this tunnel are religious texts. The "Book of the Gates." Now the "Book of the Gates" was crucial to anyone wanting to get to the next world. And pharaohs had the "Book of the Gates" carved on their tombs. It gave you the magical words to go through doorways to the next world. There would be guardians, and at each gate there would be someone else and you'd have to know the password. "The Book of the Gates" gave you those passwords. So they were crucial. And on the wall of this tunnel leading to this strange monument, we have the "Book of the Gates" inscribed by Seti, no question about it. So it seems as if Seti built this monument to Osiris perhaps and carved his name on the walls.

Now one other—along with this theory there's a kind of side theory that some people suggested, a different use for this. Built by Seti, but a different use. It's been suggested that Seti left his sarcophagus here, and all of his funerary equipment until it was time for his burial in the Valley of the Kings. That by keeping the sarcophagus and the empty canopic jars and all of that material he would associate himself with Osiris and like Osiris resurrect in the next world. So built by Seti, maybe as a cenotaph for Osiris. Maybe just to house Seti's funerary equipment until he is going to be buried. That's theory one. Most people subscribe to that. It's built by Seti I.

Let me give you theory two. My theory, so naturally this is the one that's correct. My theory is that it wasn't built by Seti I. That it's a much earlier monument. And let me give you the reasons for this theory and then you decide. First, the temple at Abydos that Seti built—not the Osireion, but the real temple, the main temple, doesn't follow the ordinary plan of an Egyptian temple. Egyptian temples are usually built on a single axis, like a railroad flat. It goes straight. First you might have the open courtyard. Then you might have the enclosed courtyard, and then you might have the holy of holies where the statue of the god was kept. But basically it's a three-part temple on a straight line. This temple at Abydos doesn't go straight. It goes straight back for a while. But then just before the Osireion, it goes left. It is shaped like an "L." Like an "L." Now why shape this temple like an "L"? My feeling, my suggestion, is that Seti was building the temple at Abydos. This ancient monument was covered over by sand. It's 30 feet below ground level. Covered over by sand. They start building the temple back, and they discover this monument. They make the temple go left and then Seti, wanting to take credit for this great ancient monument, carves his inscription on the tunnel wall leading down to the monument. So I think Seti—it's discovered in Seti's time and then claimed by Seti as his monument.

But let me give you more evidence for this. There's a little more evidence. Look at the stones. They're huge. Monolithic. If you remember I told you that; these were very very large stones. Never, never do you get that kind of building in the time of Seti I. The only monument that looks like the Osireion is the Valley Temple of King Chephren of theOld Kingdom. Same architecture. Huge stones with larger ones going across them. Only in the Valley Temple of Chephren do we get that. So I think the architecture suggests that it's a much older monument.

And let me give you one more reason for agreeing with me. There is a restoration on the Osireion. A block of granite cracked and the block was repaired, in ancient times. And the way you repair granite sometimes is by what we call a "butterfly clamp." Across the crack you carve out some thing in the shape of a butterfly. You have another little plug and you plug it in and it holds the two blocks together. But it's called a "butterfly clamp." There is one block that cracked, and it's repaired in this traditional ancient way, with a butterfly clamp. Now the block is a dark granite. And the butterfly is a light granite, and inscribed on the little butterfly insert to hold the block together is Seti's name. Now many people suggest that it shows Seti built this monument. I think it's just the opposite. If you were building something and it broke, and you had to repair it, you would repair it so you couldn't see the repair. That's what the ancient Egyptians did. They always did it so you can't see the repair. So I think the fact that Seti is repairing it with a butterfly of a different color, and then putting his name on it, he's taking credit for repairing an ancient monument. He's not building a new thing and then repairing it and putting his name on a repair. So I think, just a suggestion, that this is actually a very ancient monument, built as indeed the tomb of Osiris. But it was lost in time. Covered by sands and Seti re-discovers it. Just a theory.

But anyway Seti dies, and is buried in the Valley of the Kings. His tomb has an astronomical ceiling. It's beautiful. The goddess Nut and all the signs of the zodiac are up there. It's quite beautiful. Painted blue. But even more astounding was his sarcophagus. Translucent alabaster. And on it, the "Book of the Gates." This was discovered, I mentioned it once before, by Giovanni Belzoni, an Italian strongman who brought this sarcophagus to England to sell, and offered it to the British Museum. They refused it, and it was bought by John Soane, and it's now in the museum called the (Sir) John Soane Museum, in London, and you can see it in that museum.

But Seti, when he died, had prepared his son to become king of Egypt, and he would do it well. That son is Ramses the Great. And we'll talk about him next time.

Lecture Thirty
Ramses the Great—The Early Years

Scope:

Ramses II (the Great) ruled for 67 years and was considered one of Egypt's greatest pharaohs. We will see how this reputation rests on two areas—Ramses as warrior and Ramses as builder.

Outline

I. The early years, before Ramses became king, were promising ones.

    A. He campaigned with his father, Seti I, in Syria and is shown next to his dad's chariot.

    B. He was named "eldest son," even though he had no brothers.

    C. He is shown in the Hall of the Ancestors in the Abydos Temple helping his father, Seti I.

    D. Ramses took two chief wives, Nefertari and Istnofret. They had five sons and two daughters.

        1. Nefertari, the Great Wife, bore the Crown Prince Amunhirkepshef.

        2. Istnofret bore Khaemwaset, who became High Priest of Memphis and labeled the pyramids. He also built the Serapeum, the burial place of the Apis Bull.

        3. Istnofret also had Merneptah, the 13th of Ramses's 52 sons, who would become pharaoh.

II. The young pharaoh was very bold.

    A. Ramses's five names and epithets indicated a future military career:

        1. Horus, "Strong Bull, Beloved of Truth."

        2. Two Ladies, "Protector of Egypt Who Subdues Foreign Lands."

        3. Golden Horus, "Rich in Years, Great in Victories."

        4. King of Upper and Lower Egypt (*Usr-maat-Re*), "Strong in Right is Re."

        5. Son of Re, Ramses II, "Beloved of Amun."

        6. His own name, literally translated, is no less impressive: *Ra* = sun god; *mses* = is born.

B. Ramses completed Seti's temple at Abydos and carved his own inscription, then built a temple behind it. He also completed the Hypostyle Hall at Karnak Temple and claimed credit for it as his own.

C. The battle of Kadesh (year 5) established his reputation. Syria, controlled by Hittites, was independent of Egypt; when there was a revolt in the Levant, Ramses rode out!

    1. Four military divisions (Amun, Re, Ptah, Set) of 5,000 men each marched through Gaza to Kadesh. They took town after town. But the logistics of food and water proved to be difficult.

    2. In the official Egyptian account, two captured spies told Ramses that Muwatallis the Hittite king was fleeing. (In truth, he had 40,000 troops and 2,500 chariots hidden in the woods.)

    3. Ramses, believing the spies, proceeded ahead of his lagging army; behind him, the Division of Re was attacked.

    4. Ramses's camp was surprised by the Hittite attack, but the pharaoh rallied a few troops, counterattacked, and saved the day.

    5. Egyptian troops arrived and drove the Hittites across the Orontes River. The Prince of Aleppo, fighting with the Hittites, nearly drowned, and his predicament was ridiculed in Egyptian records.

    6. The next day Egyptians and Hittites fought to a standoff. Ramses refused a peace treaty with the Hittites, accepting only a temporary truce. He returned to Egypt.

    7. The battle account is carved everywhere—Egypt's version of *George Washington Crossing the Delaware*. Ramses is shown as larger than life, a king leading his army to save the day.

III. Ramses was unequaled as a builder.

A. He moved the administrative capital from Memphis to Pi-Ramses (Qantir) in the Delta, a more strategic location from a military point of view.

B. He built a famous temple at Abu Simbel, south of Aswan, in Nubia.

    1. He had the unique temple carved out of a mountain. It was a great piece of architectural propaganda for

Nubians sailing north on the Nile, its walls depicting bound Nubian captives.

2. Inside, the battle of Kadesh is depicted, and Ramses is shown among the gods as a statute. Twice a year, the sun illuminated the temple interior.

3. He also built a second temple, for Nefertari, with an inscription above the doorway that says, "she for whom the sun does shine."

4. Both temples were moved to higher ground by UNESCO in the 1960s when the Aswan Dam was built. They were dismantled and reassembled exactly as they would have appeared in ancient times, fallen statues and all.

5. In addition, Ramses built the Ramesseum, his mortuary temple. Percy Bysshe Shelley's "Ozymandias"—"King of Kings—look upon my monuments and despair"—is about the ruined statue at the Ramesseum. Shelley, however, had never seen it.

C. Ramses established himself as a great leader and builder. But Ramses the Great was due to have something of a midlife crisis.

Essential Reading:

K. A. Kitchen, *Pharaoh Triumphant: The Life and Times of Ramses II.*

Supplementary Reading:

Rita E. Freed, *Ramses the Great.*

Questions to Consider:

1. What really happened at the battle of Kadesh?

2. What was novel about the temple at Abu Simbel?

Lecture Thirty—Transcript
Ramses the Great—The Early Years

Hi. If you remember last time we talked about Seti I. And he's the first great king of the XIXth Dynasty. Well I mentioned before that his son is going to become Ramses the Great. One of the greatest pharaohs Egypt ever saw, and I want to talk about Ramses the Great. I want to talk about the early years. Seti of course, as all kings eventually do, dies and is buried in a beautiful tomb in the Valley of the Kings. It has a wonderful astronomical ceiling. Really quite something. But before he died, he prepared his son to become king of Egypt, and Ramses, young Ramses, young prince Ramses's early days suggest he was going to be a great king.

Now first, little Ramses—and this is not unusual—went on military campaigns with his father. Probably maybe only eight, nine years old, 10 years old, and he goes on military campaigns. He was probably kept at a safe distance. You know, a couple of soldiers around him to make sure he was okay. But he saw what fighting was about. There are scenes carved on temple walls by Seti showing young Ramses next to dad's chariot. He wasn't in the middle of battle. But it was a good picture, it was good propaganda. Now another thing that indicates that Ramses was being groomed real early to be king. If you remember, he had a brother who died. So he's the only son of Seti I. Ramses. Only son. But he's called the "Eldest Son." What that means is he's the Crown Prince. They're sort of emphasizing, this kid is going to be king of Egypt and I say he's called "Eldest Son," even though he's the only son. Also if you remember, when Seti built his temple at Abydos, the sacred city, he had a "Hall of the Ancients" where he had all the cartouches of his ancestors. And right next to Seti, performing a ritual in that hall, is young Prince Ramses, Ramses the Great. You can always tell—when he was a prince. He's got the sidelock of youth. Young children in Egypt wore a sidelock down the side of their head, and when you finally reached maturity they would cut it off, and then you became an adult. So Ramses is up and coming.

Now as a teenager, maybe probably 15, 16, something like that—he's not quite yet king yet—he took two wives. Not unusual to marry that early. He was a prince, and he has two wives. One is Nefertari. Not to be confused with Nefertiti. Nefertiti was the wife of Akhenaten, the heretic pharaoh. Nefertari is the wife of Ramses the

Great. Nefertari. It's a beautiful name. It means—"nefer" is "beautiful." or "good." And it means, "the beautiful one has come." So it's a nice name, and you'll see, by the way, Ramses really loved her. His other wife Istnofret—another nice name. Something like "the beautiful Isis." Something like that. So he has two wives— Nefertari is the honcho, the great wife, and Istnofret—and they have five sons and two daughters. Nefertari—her son, the eldest son, is the Crown Prince. Amunhirkepshef is his name. Amunhirkepshef. Names are great. Amun—the god Amun—a *kepshef* is a sword, a kind of sickle-shaped sword, and *hir* means "upon." So it's "Amun is upon my sword." This kid's going to be a warrior. Kind of a military name. Amunhirkepshef, the son by Nefertari, is going to be, hopefully, king of Egypt. Other sons by Istnofret are going to be very important kids, very important. One son—Khaemwaset—he will be the High Priest of Memphis. He will also be the first archaeologist that we know of. He is the first archaeologist in recorded history. Interesting guy. He was concerned—Khaemwaset, the son of Ramses the Great—Khaemwaset was concerned that the pyramids, which are of course ancient now, as you know; they're 1,000 years old—he was concerned that people wouldn't know who the pharaohs were who built the pyramids. So he went around labeling them.

And for example, if you remember back to the Vth Dynasty, the pyramid of Unas, the first pyramid to have pyramid texts. If you go to that pyramid, there's a big hieroglyphic inscription on the outside of the pyramid. Now most tourists, of course they can't read it and they figure it's from the time of Unas. No, it's Khaemwaset, saying, "I restored this pyramid," taking credit for it. So in a sense he creates the first museum labels in history, saying this pyramid is this guy. He also is the one who builds the Serapeum. The sacred place for the burial of the Apis bulls. At Memphis and he's High Priest at Memphis. So this is quite a kid—quite a kid, Khaemwaset. But we'll talk about him later.

Now there are other children that are important. Merneptah, a brother of Khaemwaset. Now Merneptah is only the 13th son of Ramses the Great. Ramses had a lot of kids, as you will see—he had probably 52 sons. Fifty-two sons, maybe almost an equal number of daughters. One hundred kids. A lot of wives of course. Merneptah is only the 13th son. But he's going to become king of Egypt. Ramses is going to live so long—into his 80s. He is going to rule for 67 years, that many of his children will die before him. So we have lots of important sons we know about, and Amunhirkepshef won't last long enough to become king. Khaemwaset won't. It's going to be the 13th son, Merneptah.

But let's talk about young Ramses. First when he finally does become king. Now he's trained with the military. He's gone out on campaigns with dad. He's not afraid. When he's trained with the military. But he takes his names as pharaoh—now when you're pharaoh you take new names, and every pharaoh had five names. Five. Associating himself with the different gods and goddesses. If you'll look at Ramses's names, you just know he's going to be a military man. Let's talk about the five names of Ramses the Great. First you have a Horus name. The name that associates you with the falcon god. If you'll remember, way back in the archaic period, like the First Dynasty, that was the only name pharaohs had. The "Horus name" was important, and his name is Horus "Strong Bull Beloved of Truth." So it was "Strong Bull." That's his Horus name.

The next name is called the "Two Ladies" name. Why Two Ladies? Two of the earliest goddesses Nekhbet and Wadjet (from the city of Buto.) They were a vulture and a cobra for Upper and Lower Egypt. They're called "Two Ladies." This is why on Tutankhamen's crown, for example, you will see a vulture and a cobra coming out of the forehead, protecting. Signs of royalty. So every pharaoh had a "Two Ladies" name, associating himself with these two early goddesses, and his was "Protector of Egypt Who Subdues Foreign Lands." Again military. Then there was a "Golden Horus" name, associating the king with the "Horus of gold." Ramses's "Golden Horus" name: "Rich in Years, Great in Victories." Both were true. Both would be true. He would live many years and he would win many victories. His fourth name—now we're coming to the two names that are written in cartouches—remember, only two of these five names are written in cartouches. One is the name that says he's king of Upper and Lower Egypt: "Strong in Right is Re." That's his name: "Strong In Right Is Re." Powerful—that's the image he wants to give. That name, by the way, in Egyptian: "Usr-maat-Re"—strong in might. "Usr-maat-Re." Remember it. You'll see why in a little bit. "Usr-maat-Re," and then his last name, also written in a cartouche which says "Son of Re." He's the son of the Sun God. Ramses II, Beloved of Amun. Ramses beloved of Amun. Ramses beloved of Amun. Those are his five names. Powerful names.

The name Ramses by the way—Ramses. Ra is the Sun God. "Mses" is born. "Ra is born." That's what his name means. That's why you have so many pharaohs named with "Mosis" at the end. Tuthmosis— "Toth is born." Mosis—the moon god. All of these are typical Egyptian names. The gods are born. This is why when we talk about the Exodus later, you will see that the name Moses is not a Hebrew name. It's pure Egyptian. It means birth. But we'll talk about the Exodus later.

So Ramses had these five names. Powerful man. But it's not just names. He builds. He fights. He does everything. The first thing he does is complete his father's temple at Abydos. Seti died before it was completed. So Ramses goes to the sacred city and completes his father's temple. But he does something quite interesting, which shows his ego. The temple of Seti was dedicated to many gods if you remember. So it had quite a few doorways. Ramses bricks up these doorways. Bricks them up with stone. So he'll have room to carve his own name on the doorways, and carve his exploits on the doorways of his father's temple, and says it is a good son who completes his father's monument. So in a sense he completes his father's monument, but takes a lot of credit for himself. So he goes to Abydos and completes his father's temple. But he also builds his own temple at Abydos, behind dad's. So he's got his own temple there. He also completes the Hypostyle Hall at Karnak temple that Seti his father had begun. And if you go to the Hypostyle Hall today, you will see it with Ramses's name on it. You're not going to see Seti's name all over it. Ramses loved to put his own name. We sometimes call Ramses "The Great Chiseler" because he carved out so many other kings' names and put his own on. We call him "The Great Chiseler." But he builds.

Now military—that's where it's at for Ramses. Year five of his reign, his fifth year as king of Egypt, he marches out to Syria. This is going to be the battle that will make his reputation for life. Now Ramses is going to rule for another 62 years. Rules for 67 years. But in the fifth year of his reign, he fights a battle that he will talk about for another six decades—the battle of Kadesh. It's in Syria, and as I mentioned, his father had gone there and conquered. It's a long march, as you know from when we talked about the military. It's about 15 miles a day, marching to Syria. You go through the Beka valley. You see flowers these guys had never seen before. New wild flowers. We have the details of this battle.

Let me tell you about this battle. Ramses talked about it so much, carved it on so many temples, that it's the best recorded event in ancient history. There is no other historical event of which we have so much detail and so many accounts.

Ramses really liked it. He's marching out. He of course isn't marching., he's in his chariot. The infantry is marching and there were four military divisions we are told. We know they divided themselves into military divisions. They are named after the gods. There's one for Amun. One for Re. One for Ptah. So we have Amun for Thebes. Re is the solar God. Ptah for Memphis, the other capital of Egypt. And Seth. Seth. Remember his father is Seti I. So Seth is taken care of too. We have four divisions. Five thousand men each. So we've got about 20,000. We've got chariots. We've got archers, and they're marching north to Syria. Town after town they go through, they simply take. No resistance. No problem for an army like this.

And understand, moving 20,000 men is not easy. Anybody in the military knows that. You've got supply problems—that's the big one. How do you feed 20,000? You can't carry enough food. If you're moving with donkeys as your pack animal, a donkey can carry maybe enough food for two days for itself and its rider. No way. You have to forage where you're going. Take whatever the land has, and that's what they did. So they're marching north. Even wells are a problem. You know, if you have an army of 20,000 and you come to a town where there are four wells, you'll die of thirst. You cannot water 20,000 people quickly enough from a few wells. So you had to know what you were doing, and you planned your time. So he's marching north—to Kadesh.

Now Ramses is nearing Kadesh, and it's a dramatic story. Told by Ramses. We don't know exactly what the truth is. But let me give you the official Egyptian account, and then we'll talk about it. Ramses was leading his army. Now he's young. Remember year five. You know, he was—23, who knows how old, 24, max?—and he's leading the army. He's been out on campaigns, so he's not afraid. He's leading the army and they're nearing Kadesh. As they near Kadesh, two locals come up to him. Join the camp. Two locals and they say to Ramses, we want to join your camp. They want to join Ramses's camp. And Ramses has them interrogated and he says, where is the enemy?

Now the enemy, Muwatallis, he's king of the Hittites. The Hittites controlled Kadesh all the way from Turkey. They controlled Syria. He says, where's the enemy? And these two guys say, well, they heard you were coming, Ramses, and they fled north. They're 100 miles north. In truth, Muwatallis had 40,000 troops. Twenty-five-hundred chariots hidden in the woods. A little bit north. Near Kadesh. Ramses believes these guys. It makes sense to him. "They're afraid of me!" and he proceeds ahead of his army.

Now when you've got 20,000 men, you can't march together. It's too many. You usually divide up among divisions. And you've got maybe 5,000 moving ahead. That's plenty, and they sometimes camp as much as a day apart. Because they've got to get their own food, water. You can't just supply everybody at once. Ramses, hearing that the enemy is not near, charges on ahead on his own. He's got one division with him, and he's marching to Kadesh.

What Ramses doesn't know of course is, Muwatallis is waiting. Waiting. Ramses goes on ahead. Behind him, the division of Re is attacked. They're in real trouble. Ramses marching on, sets up camp. And we have descriptions of what happened. We have pictures of the camp that Ramses actually set up. Remember I told you once before, they put up their Egyptian shields to form a wall. That's what they did, and it's a wonderful scene on the walls. You can see guys repairing chariots, carrying supplies. You can see Ramses's pet lion—he went into battle with his lion. They're setting up camp and they find two spies sent by Muwatallis, and they beat the truth out of these guys and learn that Muwatallis is in the woods.

But it's too late. The Hittites attack the camp and it's all confusion. They're not ready for battle. They're outnumbered. Everybody is scattering. Ramses says what are you, afraid? He says, "I'll fight them by myself!" and he jumps in his chariot and he counterattacks the Hittites. Now we don't know exactly what happens. The description is pretty much that Ramses, with very few people behind him, repels the Hittites. Ramses saves the day. Everybody is panicking and Ramses says, don't worry. I've got Amun behind me, and he charges. The Hittites retreat. And there were even scenes of the Hittites retreating. Wonderful. Now remember this is Kadesh. In Syria. They're right near the Orontes River, and the Hittites are pushed back across the Orontes by Ramses. And there's a scene on a temple wall that Ramses later carved of a prince of Aleppo in Syria who was fighting with the Hittites, and the guy almost drowned in the river, and it shows them holding him upside down so the water's coming out of him. They're shaking the water out of this prince of Aleppo.

So anyway, Ramses saves the day. The rest of the troops come north and join the camp. Now it's nightfall. Egyptians did not fight battles at night. In the ancient world in general, you did not fight at night. So you're going to wait for the next day. But at least now Ramses and his troops, they know that Muwatallis is there on the other side of the river. Day breaks, and there is a battle between the Egyptians and the Hittite forces for Kadesh. The best that we can determine from the records we have, and it's only one-sided, is it was a stand-off. Muwatallis had the numbers. Had outnumbered Ramses. Ramses's men were really trained. Skilled. It was a stand-off. Nobody won. There are scenes of the battle and there are ways of telling the good guys from the bad guys. Remember I told you once, about the round topped shields of the Egyptians. Well chariots also. Egyptians always have two guys on a chariot, Hittites have three. They've got a bigger chariot, they have a spear thrower too. So you can tell pretty clearly who's who, what's happening. And it was a stand-off, and Ramses is offered a peace treaty. He refuses. He won't take a peace treaty. He will only take a temporary truce.

Now what's the difference? Well one is a long-term thing where you say, well, we're not going to fight anymore. We're going to do this, we're going to do that. Ramses says no. He said, we'll take a truce. But I'm going to be back. So Ramses refuses a treaty and returns to Egypt. Now this is a battle that becomes the equivalent of "George Washington crossing the Delaware." It is carved on every temple Ramses builds. It is spoken about for years, about how Ramses as an individual, the king leading his army, saved the day. And it's probably—there's probably some truth in it. There is. Because there were a lot of soldiers coming back with Ramses and if he hadn't done something pretty brave there would have been talk. So I think Ramses really did do something great. Maybe not as great as he said. But it's good. So Ramses early on in his career establishes himself as a great military leader.

Now what about his building? There were various ways a pharaoh wanted to show he was great—one of the strategic things Ramses does, and it's important, is he moves the capital of Egypt. Now remember there are two capitals really. Thebes is the religious capital. And Thebes, by the way, is what the Greeks called it. That's not what the Egyptians called it. The Egyptians called ancient Thebes *Waset*. It's a scepter. It means power. It was the place of power. *Waset*. So the ancient Egyptians called it *Waset*. The Greeks, when they came in, called it Thebes and the modern Egyptians call it Luxor. There was the religious capital at Thebes and the administrative capital at Memphis. But Ramses moves the administrative capital from Memphis to the Delta—now why? To modern Qantir actually. The ancient city is called Pi-Ramses. The city of Ramses. Why? Because the Delta is more strategic if you're a military man. It's difficult to imagine what being a military man was like. I mean, you had to plan for going through deserts. Marching endlessly, and if you're going through the Delta you can have "store cities" built there. It's a place where you can move out north towards Syria. And Ramses intended to go to Syria often. So it was strategically better placed for a military man. That's why he wants his capital in the Delta. It's a strange area to see today because you know the Delta is moist, so most of the site has sunken under ground. You can still see places where Ramses built, though. It's amazing. Big stones still lie on the ground.

But anyway, in addition to a new capital, he builds a famous temple at Abu Simbel. Now if you'll remember, the border of Egypt ended at Aswan in the south. Ended there. Abu Simbel is south of Aswan, in Nubia. In Nubia, and Abu Simbel—which is the modern name for it—Abu Simbel is a unique temple. Nothing like it had ever been built. Ramses has a new technique. Normally, a temple is built out of blocks. Built one on top of the other. Very much like you build a brick house. Ramses carved the temple of Abu Simbel out of the mountain. Out of the living rock. In the front of this temple carved out of the mountain are four 67-foot high statues of Ramses the Great—four of them. And you enter the temple between the legs of the inner-most two.

When you look at the temple today one of the statue's heads is on the ground. It fell during an earthquake. During the life of Ramses. After it had been built, there was an earthquake and the head fell down. Now this temple is a great piece of propaganda. Let me explain why I say propaganda. No large number of people ever lived there. This was Nubia, not Egyptian soil. Egyptians weren't going to live there for a long time. This was to show, if you were a Nubian sailing northward on the Nile in to Egypt, you would have to pass this big big temple with 67-foot statues of Ramses looking down on you. Now, if you were brave enough to get off your boat and look around inside the temple, as you go inside the temple—right on the walls, just at the entranceway—are carved bound captives. Nubians. It's a statement. It's a political statement. Then, if you're brave enough to go inside you will see Ramses winning the battle of Kadesh. Wonderful scenes. The Orontes River circling the town, pretty impressive stuff.

And then, going all the way in to the holy of holies, what do you have? You have four statues of the gods. You have Re-Horakhty, you have Ptah, you have Amun. And you have Ramses the Great. Right there. With the gods. Same size. So you've got Ramses as a god. And the temple is designed beautifully, so that twice a year the sun shines all the way into the holy of holies and illuminates the statues. Special day. Many people feel that it was on Ramses's birthday. It was designed so that on Ramses's birthday, the sun would illuminate those statues of Ramses with the gods. Incredible.

Now to build this temple was a major effort. Nothing like it had ever been done. Imagine how they did it. You had to have guys on scaffolds coming from the top of the mountain and they would put down a grid work. They would take big buckets probably of red paint. Paint the red line. The grid and then the sculptors would come, hanging, and carve out these statues. All for propaganda. But this is not the only temple there. Ramses also built a second temple. Just to the right of it. for his wife Nefertari. The beautiful Nefertari. And above the doorway is a lovely inscription. It says, "Nefertari. She for whom the sun does shine." It's nice, isn't it? So they have his-and-her temples, sort of his-and-her temples at Abu Simbel. It's amazing.

Also, by the way you should know that these temples were moved by UNESCO. Remember when the Aswan Dam was built, it backed up the waters of the Nile forming Lake Nasser and Abu Simbel was going to be flooded. So many countries combined under UNESCO to move the temple, rather than lose it under water, and they cut it into blocks. Large blocks. You know like 20-ton blocks. And these blocks were moved to higher ground. It's on the same spot, so to speak. On the mainland of the Nile, same spot. Just higher up. And it's positioned, by the way, so that the sun still shines in on the same days on Ramses the Great. It's quite a temple. It's really something.

And by the way there was an interesting discussion when they were moving the temple. What do you do about the head that's on the ground? Should you put it back? They could have put it back. They could have had metal rods to pin it on. They decided to leave the head still on the ground. The one fallen head of the four statues, because that's the way it was in ancient times. And that's the way they were going to leave it. So the head is still on the ground. And when you visit the temple—and you all should visit it—you can't even see the lines where they cut the blocks. They did such a good job of moving the temple. It's hard to see that it was rebuilt. But that's one temple that Ramses the Great built.

Now another important monument that he builds is the "Ramesseum" as it's called; his mortuary temple. It's where Ramses would be worshipped for centuries to come. And what's important about this temple, is that he had a colossal statue there. Big, big statue out of granite. Beautiful statue. But it's terribly ruined. Overthrown by an earthquake probably. But this is the statue in the Ramesseum that Percy Bysshe Shelley wrote his poem "Ozymandias" about. He wrote about the "king of kings." "Look upon my monuments and despair." The idea is that, I was pretty great, but look at my monument. All that's left is this visage, this face. This is the statue that Shelley wrote about.

But, you know, Shelley had never seen it. He'd never been to Egypt. He'd never seen the statue. He'd only heard about it. But he wrote a wonderful poem about it. And the reason it's called "Ozymandias"—if you'll remember, Ramses's name was "Usr-maat-Re"—it was a Greek corruption. They heard "Usr-maat-Re," and they said "Ozymandias," and that's how Shelley wrote the name. So Ramses the Great became "Ozymandias" of the famous poem.

So Ramses, early in his career, establishes himself as a great builder. The Ramesseum. Abu Simbel. He builds his own temple at Abydos. Completes the Hypostyle Hall at Karnak. Completes his father's temple at Abydos. Does it all. Marches out to Kadesh. Holds off the Hittite army singlehandedly. He's established. But this is only the beginning of his career. Something happens, almost a midlife crisis, that changes Ramses's career radically. But we'll talk about that next time. See you then.

Lecture Thirty-One
Ramses the Great—The Later Years

Scope:

There is a bit of a mystery about Ramses's reign—his personality seems to have changed from the great warrior/builder to a more sedentary pharaoh. Today, we would call it a midlife crisis. We will discuss the last 40 years of Ramses's reign and see how they differed from the glorious beginning. We will also see how a pharaoh with the resources of Ramses prepared his family for the next world.

Outline

I. Ramses's days as a warrior were limited to his earliest years.

   A. In year 8, Ramses rode out to Syria and, although successful, he did not take Kadesh nor make a permanent conquest of the region.

   B. Because Egypt never had an occupying army in Syria, repeated campaigns were necessary to gain tribute.

   C. The Hittite peace treaty (year 21) told a great deal about Ramses.

      1. The Hittites, weakened by fighting both Assyrians and Egyptians, needed a treaty.

      2. It was first written on a silver tablet in cuneiform and then rewritten in hieroglyphs on the walls of the Karnak and Abu Simbel temples.

      3. The treaty, perhaps the first written down in history, contained defense and trade agreements and a nonaggression pact. Ramses, who didn't seem to have any fight left in him, accepted.

   D. Ramses took a Hittite bride (year 34), which suggests he wanted peace.

      1. He boasted of her dowry (silver, gold, horses, minerals): "Greater will her dowry be than that of the daughter of the King of Babylon."

      2. It was an 800-mile trip, and the bride came with an escort.

      3. Hittite and Egyptian soldiers "ate and drank face to face, not fighting," according to an inscription on a temple wall. This was amazing! Hittites were one of Egypt's nine traditional enemies.

E. Huttusilis II, king of the Hittites, asked for an Egyptian physician for his sister who couldn't have children, yet another indication of a new friendship between rivals. Egyptian medicine had such specialists as gynecologists and eye doctors.

F. Ramses took a second Hittite bride (year 44) to further establish peace. Ramses, it would seem, was mellowing.

II. Ramses experienced several major deaths in the family.

A. Nefertari died as Abu Simbel was completed (year 20). Her death wasn't formally announced; we know of it because she merely disappears from the historical record.

B. First-born son Amunhirkepshef, the crown prince, died in around year 17.

C. Khaemwaset, the overachiever son who labeled the pyramids, died and is perhaps buried in the Serapeum.

III. Ramses became the tomb builder. No more great temples—he looked instead toward death.

A. Nefertari's tomb in the Valley of the Queens is the most beautiful of all, restored by the Getty Institute by removing salt crystals beneath the plaster before replastering. Today, visitors to the tomb are limited, because their presence—as in any tomb—affects the humidity.

B. KV 5, the tomb of Ramses's sons, is the largest in Egypt. He did have 52 sons!

   1. Found early in the 19th century and later lost, the tomb was rediscovered (in 1987) by Dr. Kent Weeks's Theban Mapping Project.

   2. It's the largest tomb in all of Egypt. The architecture, with hundreds of rooms on several levels, is unique. Perhaps some of the rooms were chapels for offerings to the sons. It may take over a century to excavate KV 5 safely.

C. Ramses's tomb is a reflection of his greatness.

   1. The workmen's village at Deir el Medineh was supported by Ramses just to build tombs. We know more about this town than about any other ancient city in the world.

2. Because of this town, we know how to build a royal tomb. There were two gangs, one left-hand and one right-hand, working simultaneously. Bronze chisels were weighed at the beginning and end of the week so no one could steal any bronze. An entire city was erected to work on the tombs of Ramses and his sons.

3. The burial chamber of Ramses the Great probably held more treasure than any other single room in antiquity.

D. Why did Ramses have a midlife crisis? The Exodus, as we shall see in the next lecture, may have had something to do with it.

Essential Reading:

K. A. Kitchen, *Pharaoh Triumphant: The Life and Times of Ramses II.*

Supplementary Reading:

Rita E. Freed, *Ramses the Great.*

Questions to Consider:

1. What events suggest a change in Ramses's personality?

2. Why is the tomb of Ramses considered so extraordinary?

Lecture Thirty-One—Transcript
Ramses the Great—The Later Years

Welcome back. Remember last time we were talking about Ramses the Great. And I mentioned that Ramses is one of my favorite personalities of all of Egyptian history. I think there's really two reasons for that. One is, he's a great guy. But the other is, we have an awful lot of information about him, so we can know something about him. And he gets to become a human being.

He ruled for 67 years. So that's plenty of time to build up a kind of dossier, a resumé. And last time we talked about the early years. And the two things I stressed was one, Ramses as a warrior. Remember the battle of Kadesh in year five. He marches out and fights the Hittites at Kadesh. He doesn't win, but he certainly distinguishes himself. He holds off the troops—by himself, he says. And eventually at the end he was offered a peace treaty, and he refuses it. He's only willing to take a truce. Because he's going to be back. So Ramses is a warrior. There's no question about it. At least, in his early years.

Then I also tried to show Ramses as a builder. Remember, he built the incredible temple at Abu Simbel with those 67-foot high statues of himself. It was a great piece of propaganda. So that anybody coming north from Nubia would have to go right by it. And you'd see these statues of Ramses. And then if you got off the boat and you went inside the temple, what do you see? Nubians as bound captives. Pretty impressive stuff.

But that was Ramses in the early years. I want to talk about the later years today. There's a bit of a mystery about Ramses. After this incredible start, really kind of an aggressive start, you know—going to build, going to fight—Ramses has what we might call today a mid-life crisis. His personality changes radically. He becomes more sedentary, and we're not exactly sure why. But today I want to trace the latter years of my man Ramses the Great. And I also want to show you, how when you rule for 67 years and you're a powerful pharaoh, what kind of resources are available to you to build your tomb in the Valley of the Kings. You see, we're all familiar with Tutankhamen's tomb, because that had all the goodies stuffed in it. But Tutankhamen was a relatively minor king, ruling for only 10 years. What about Ramses, who's Ramses the Great? And rules for

67 years? So we'll talk about how a pharaoh with real resources can prepare for the next life.

But let's start with Ramses as a warrior. Now Kadesh is behind him. He's distinguished himself at the battle of Kadesh. He has carved it on temple walls. Everybody knows he's a great warrior. But he marches out again in year eight. He marches out to Syria again. Once again he's going to Syria. A long haul. And he does pretty well. I mean it's successful. But he doesn't conquer Kadesh. He comes back. But he hasn't conquered Kadesh, which is an interesting thing. Now the reason he had to march out again, and the Egyptians marched out again and again and again was that—remember, they never had an occupying force. When they conquered a country, they didn't leave say a garrison of 2,000 soldiers to make sure these people stayed in line and paid their taxes or whatever. No. The Egyptians never wanted to live on foreign soil. Because if they died on foreign soil, they might not be mummified and they'd lose their chance at immortality. So because they never left a kind of colony in any country, they had to go back every year if they wanted the tribute. And that's what happens. Ramses marches out again and again.

In year eight, he goes to Syria. He does okay, but doesn't capture Kadesh. Now in year 21 of Ramses's reign—he's been reigning for 21 years now. He's in his 40s. Just about in his 40s. He signs a treaty with the Hittite king. He signs the Hittite treaty. Now remember at Kadesh he wasn't willing to sign a treaty. It's, no, maybe a temporary truce. And the treaty is an interesting document. The Hittites really needed it; they needed this treaty. They were fighting the Assyrians and they couldn't really battle Assyrians and Egyptians at the same time. So it's understandable from the Hittite point of view. We need a treaty. But this is just the very time when Ramses, you might think, would march out and defeat the Hittites. They've divided their forces, they've got to fight the Assyrians. They're going to fight us. But no. Ramses accepts it. For some reason in the 21st year of Ramses's reign, this great warrior says "no more war."

It's a very interesting document, by the way. We don't have the original version of it that the Hittites sent. But the Egyptians were pretty impressed with it. It came on a silver tablet. It was a silver tablet. Inscribed in cuneiform. Now, cuneiform is not a language— it's a script. In other words, all "cuneiform" means is "wedged-shaped writing." So it was usually done with a stylus. You had a little triangular stylus, and you impressed it on something, usually clay. And that's cuneiform. But you could write in many languages in this script, in the same way we use the exact same letters for French, Spanish, and English. A "T" still looks like a "T." It's the same with cuneiform. You could use cuneiform for lots of different languages. So the people who lived in the Mesopotamian city of Akkad, they wrote in Akkadian. The Sumerians, who lived in Sumer, in southern Mesopotamia wrote in Sumerian. But they all used the same letters, the cuneiform script.

So this tablet, the silver tablet comes to Ramses the Great. And the Egyptians, when they wrote their translation of it, Ramses put it on temple walls—it's on the wall at Abu Simbel, his temple that he built with the huge statues. It's on the wall at Karnak Temple, the Vatican of ancient Egypt. So he has several versions of this treaty that he translated. And one of the things he says in it is that it came on a silver tablet with seals and stuff. So they were kind of impressed with just the way it looked. It looked like a different kind of document for them.

Now it has everything that you would expect from a superpower agreement. Two superpowers making an agreement. It's got a non-aggression pact—I'm not going to go on your territory, you don't go on mine. It's got mutual support clauses—if I'm attacked you'll help me, if you're attacked I'll help you. It's got even trade agreements. I think it's probably the first peace treaty in the history of the world that we have. I mean it's a real document. Just to give you a feeling for it, I'll read you one little part of it. And you'll get a feeling for how these guys talked about "let's make peace."

Now remember the Hittites—the land of the Hittites was called "Hatti"—that's where we get Hittites from. "The great ruler of Hatti shall never trespass against the land of Egypt to take anything from it. Ramses shall never trespass against the land of Hatti to take anything from it. If some other foe should come against the territories of Ramses, and he sends word to the great ruler of Hatti, saying come with me as an ally against him, then the great ruler of Hatti shall act with him and shall slay his foes. And so shall Ramses for Hattusilis." (That's the king.) "As for him who shall keep to these terms on this silver tablet Hittites or Egyptians, the thousands of gods of Hatti and the thousands of gods of Egypt will cause him to flourish, will make him to live, together with his household with land and his servants." So if you follow this treaty, be you a noble or the king, you're going to prosper. So it's an important document. And I think in a sense it marks a turning for Ramses's career. He's not ready to do battle anymore. He's turned from a hawk to a dove essentially. And you might wonder why. Quite interesting.

Now the next sign that Ramses has really changed, kind of mellowed in his old age, comes in year 34. He's in his 50s now. And Ramses marries a Hittite princess. A Hittite. I mean these guys were the enemies up until the treaty. Now he's marrying a Hittite princess. This is usually done not out of love. He undoubtedly never saw her when he made the deal. You know, this is 800 miles in the north, in modern Turkey. But it cements a deal, it sort of puts the two countries on a kind of equal footing. And he's going to marry a Hittite princess. And he talks about her dowry. Now Ramses kind of has to boast no matter what happens. So for example if he's going to sign a treaty, it's out of his magnanimous gesture that he's letting this poor guy from the Hittites sign a treaty with him. Same with this princess, the Hittite bride. He says her dowry will be greater than the king of Babylon's daughter. So this is big time. And it was a big dowry. Undoubtedly. I mean Egypt was the power in the Middle East. So when this young girl, probably—she's got to be a beauty, or else she's not going to be sent—when this young girl comes to Ramses, she is coming with gold and silver and horses and jewels. I mean she's coming with stuff. And it's a long haul. It's 800 miles, roughly. So she is coming with an entourage. This is going to be an armed guard. This is a major event. A Hittite princess coming to marry Ramses the Great.

And you know, one of the things that you got out of a deal like this, was things that you didn't have. For example Egypt did not have precious stones. That's a common misconception. There is not a single precious stone in Egypt. There are no diamond, ruby, emerald mines at all. But not only that, there were certain kinds of semi-precious stones that Egypt didn't have, for example, lapis. And these guys could come with lapis. So a marriage like this was a source of things not easily acquired. A source of the luxuries that make life worth living. So Ramses was pretty happy about this deal, we can be sure. And he even carved an inscription on his temple about this marriage. And you know what amazed everybody the most? He describes the bride coming and he's pleased with her, she's more beautiful than anything, this is just kind of stock stuff. You had to say it. You know, to show that Ramses was really getting a good deal. Remember he always had his favorite wife, Nefertari. I mean she was really the apple of his eye. I mean if you'll remember over the temple at Abu Simbel he said "Nefertari, she for whom the sun doth shine." I mean, Nefertari was really his sweetie. And she's not bothered by this young princess coming. She's not bothered. This is a political marriage. But he had to say she was beautiful.

But the thing that really amazed them all—and he wrote it on the temple wall—it says, "Hittite soldiers and Egyptian soldiers sat down to eat, face to face, not fighting." I mean, it was amazing, that—a pparently all the soldiers were amazed at this—for years, the Hittites had been the traditional enemies. And here you are. The princess has come. And obviously with a small army to guard her. And now this Hittite army is banqueting with the Egyptian army, "face to face, not fighting," was the phrase. And it was incredible. Egypt had nine traditional enemies. They were called the "nine bows." And you know, the Hittites were one of them. And I'll tell you something neat. When you go to a museum, if you look at a statue of a king of this period, the New Kingdom, as we call it—and if the statue is a seated statue, where the king or queen is seated—look beneath the feet. Usually what you see beneath the feet of the statue are nine bows. In other words, the pharaoh was seated stepping on the enemy. It's a kind of symbolic gesture. But when you go to any museum, to an Egyptian collection, look at the feet of a king's statue. And you'll very often see nine bows. It's not clear what they are. But now that you know you'll see oh yeah. They're bows. Bows. From bow and arrow. So this is a big deal for the Hittite army to be eating with the Egyptian army and they're not slugging it out. It was a big deal.

There's another indication, by the way, that Ramses is softening. At least certainly to the Hittites. And he doesn't march out against anyone else either. The king of the Hittites sends a letter to Ramses. Hattusilis is the king's name. Now remember, Ramses is going to reign for 67 years. That is a long haul. So he's going to outlive an awful lot of Hittite kings, Syrian kings. He's going to outlive everybody. So the new king writes him. And says, "You know, my sister can't have children. Can't conceive. Will you send me an Egyptian physician to see if he could help with this problem?" Now again, Egypt of course, was viewed as having the best of all physicians. You remember in Egypt medicine was called "The Necessary Art." And they were, as far as I know, the first to have specialists. For example, they had eye doctors. They had gynecologists—men who specialized in women's diseases. And they were usually men who were physicians. We know of one woman physician,an interesting woman. And I think her name is Peshat. She was in the Old Kingdom, during the time of Sneferu, way back when in the Old Kingdom. And she was a royal physician. So in the early part, there was a woman who was the royal physician. But almost always the physicians are men. So because Egypt has these specialists, gynecologists perhaps, this man could help the sister conceive. So just the fact that the Hittite king is writing to Ramses and says, "hey, old boy, send me a physician." Ramses's reply is great. I mean he is funny. He says basically, "I know your sister. She's 50 if she's a day. But I'll send a physician anyway."

It is also interesting that since the woman can't conceive, the assumption of course is that it's her fault. That the reason she's not having children is the woman's problem. You don't know exactly what they really thought about conception. How did it happen? It was a relatively mysterious event, occurrence. Even until the Middle Ages in our time, our Middle Ages, conception wasn't really fully understood. I mean that's why midwives were sometimes used; it was the kind of thing that women did. You had midwives, and it was a woman's thing. And midwives weren't that well educated very often. So conception is a curious thing. So it wasn't until—and I think that's probably where you get witches becoming more important than warlocks, or whatever the male counterpart is, because women did these cunning things having to do with birth. And stuff like that. And they had their own realm. So midwives were looked at a little suspiciously. But this physician is going to be sent and he'll do what he can do. We have no idea what happens. Undoubtedly nothing. But the physician is sent.

So Ramses is mellow. The Hittite king is kind of very happy with him. They're getting along. And in year 44 or so of Ramses's reign—Ramses is now in his 60s. But think about it—he'd been ruling for 44 years. He's got another 23 years to go or so. And he's going to keep going. Anyway, in year 44 he marries another Hittite princess. Takes another one. I think this further establishes peace. What we're getting is, this is so established that these two countries are at peace with each other. Two Hittite brides. Sending physicians.

Treaties on the temple walls. I mean think about it. You carved a treaty on a temple wall; it was up there forever. It wasn't like a piece of paper, you could put it away and forget about it. So I think Ramses is mellowing. And it may not be just old age, you know, because it started fairly early.

Now let me say some things about Ramses's personal life. Not just his political aspirations, or lack of. Ramses experienced a lot of deaths, as in deaths in his family. Understand this, he had about 100 children. He actually had more than one wife. You know, he had two great ones—he had Nefertari; he had another great important wife, Istnofret. Loads of wives. Had something like 52 sons. And if you have that many children in an ancient country where death is not unusual at an early age, you're going to experience a death probably every year. One of your kids, one of your wives is going to die. And Ramses had a lot of personal tragedy. I mean you can't think about it, "Oh, he's got 100 kids, so it doesn't matter." Certainly there are people who care. People who matter to Ramses. And he's experiencing them. And I think the big one happens around year 20 of his reign. His beloved Nefertari dies.

She dies just about the time that they make their trip to Abu Simbel to dedicate the temples. Now remember at Abu Simbel, which is south of Egypt's border at Aswan, Ramses built not one temple, but two. One is his great temple where he's shown. The four statues, the 67-foot-high statues. But as you're facing it from the water, to the right is Nefertari's temple. He builds an entire huge temple, carved out of the mountain for Nefertari, where he puts this wonderful inscription "she for whom the sun doth shine." Well they complete the temples about Ramses's 20th year. And Nefertari makes the trip down, and we never hear about her again—which means she died. You don't get a formal announcement—"the queen is dead, the king is dead." You never get that. Or "the prince is dead." That never happens. In a sense it was viewed as darkness triumphing over light. So you didn't really talk about it. The way we figure out when somebody dies is when they disappear from the historical record. And after year 20, there's no more Nefertari. So that's a big blow to Ramses undoubtedly. It's interesting, by the way, that right after her death he signed the Hittite treaty. All right. She dies in year 20. And the Hittite treaty is signed around year 21. So there may be a connection between the two events. It may have taken some steam out of his sails. Maybe.

Let me tell you a funny thing about Abu Simbel, by the way, because that's a source of our information about Ramses. Now I can't prove this, I'm just sort of saying it off the top of my head. But my bet is, that Mt. Rushmore was patterned after Abu Simbel. That you've got these colossal heads of our presidents carved into a mountain. I would bet that Mt. Rushmore—really, the inspiration for it comes from Abu Simbel. Interestingly, by the way, it took the same number of years roughly to complete the two monuments. Abu Simbel and Mt. Rushmore. Though there's a difference. I mean it's not—to be fair, Mt. Rushmore is like granite. And this is a softer stone in Egypt. But to be fair, also we had pneumatic tools, we had drills and things like that. But I think Mt. Rushmore may have been inspired by Ramses the Great. Great men have great monuments.

But Nefertari is not the only one to die during Ramses's reign of course. Remember Ramses's firstborn son? Amunhirkepshef was his name. And the name means, "Amun is upon my sword." A *kepshef* is a kind of sickle sword. So it shows also that Amun is an important god. Well, Amunhirkepshef, who is really what we would call the crown prince, he's the eldest son who hopefully will eventually become king—he dies. We think around year 17 of Ramses's reign. So a little before Nefertari. Now the reason is, when various announcements are sent out to the world about various events, it almost always includes "and the king's eldest son is." And Amunhirkepshef is no longer the king's eldest son in later announcements. So we think Ramses loses his firstborn son sometime just before the completion of Abu Simbel, around year 17. Another blow to Ramses undoubtedly. The crown prince has to be the apple of dad's eye, because he's being groomed to become king of Egypt. So this was a blow.

There are other blows to Ramses. For example, remember the son Khaemwaset? Now his name means something like "rising in Thebes"or "shining in Thebes." Remember, Thebes was called *Waset*, that was the ancient name for it, meaning the scepter—power. And Khaemwaset was that overachiever son that we talked about last time. He is the first archaeologist in history. He puts labels on pyramids because he's afraid that the builders of the pyramids— now, the pyramids are of course 1,000 years old now—and he's afraid that the builders of the pyramids will be forgotten. That we won't know who built this pyramid, who built that. Because remember, most of the pyramids are uninscribed until we get to the

Vth Dynasty. So he goes around putting labels, museum labels, on pyramids. So he's really an archaeologist. But he's also the High Priest of Memphis. And that's a very important title. Memphis is the capital of Egypt now. The administrative capital is in the north. Memphis. Thebes is in the south. And Khaemwaset does other things, remember. He also is the one who starts building the Serapeum, this maze of tombs for the Apis bulls. But we'll talk about that in detail later. But Khaemwaset is really, you know, a doer. He dies also.

So we're getting an awful lot of deaths in Ramses's family, which is quite normal when you have 100 kids, God knows how many wives. You're going to experience these things. And some of them are going to be very close to you, and you're going to feel it. So I tend to get the feeling of Ramses as a man who's taken his knocks. You know the famous Mel Brooks line; "It's great to be king." Sometimes it's not so great to be king. Now Ramses turns his attention, I think, away from building temples. I mean he's a great builder; it's in his blood. But I think he turns it towards building tombs. This is where Ramses's sort of mindset is. In the next world, towards death.

And the first thing I'd like to talk about with Ramses as a tomb builder is Nefertari's tomb. His beloved wife, who dies around year 20. She's buried in the Valley of the Queens. The ancient name for the Valley of the Queens was "the place of beauty." And Nefertari's tomb, I think everybody agrees, is perhaps the most beautiful tomb in all of Egypt. It's interesting trying to figure out why. You know it's not clear. I think it's partly that the background is painted a very clear white. Most tombs don't have this white background. But it's certainly beautiful. And it was restored. You know, there are problems with the tombs in the Valley of the Kings and the Valley of the Queens. The problem is salt—salt crystals. You know, the water table has changed in Egypt since the Aswan Dam. Water is rising. It goes up into the stone. And what happens is, salt in the stone migrates to the surface in the form of crystals. And it breaks through the plaster—the painting. And the plaster starts to flake off.

Well, we were fortunate with the tomb of Nefertari, which was in terrible shape. The most beautiful tomb in Egypt was closed for many, many years. And then the Getty Institute—you know, John Paul Getty's famous museum, also has a conservation division. And they do things around the world. Gratis. For free. Just because it's a good thing to do. And you know, thank God they've got more money than anybody. And they went and for years they had a team of Italians, mainly, working on the tomb of Nefertari. They basically took the plaster off the wall and piece by piece picked out the salt crystals that had migrated to the surface, then put on a sealant, and then put the plaster back. I mean a remarkable job. And then the question was—the big debate—should we paint in the places that are missing? And they did a kind of interesting experiment. They had a section of the tomb where they put in the painting that was missing. They could have done it so you'd never know. They could have done it just like the Egyptians and you'd never be able to see it. But they decided not to. So whenever they put in a restoration they'd put a little crosshatching. Very fine. It's just that you can tell, this is new. And eventually they decided not to do it with the whole tomb. Because they decided to just restore it as best they could. And it's now open to the public. It's not easy to get in.

And in this sense—first of all it's an expensive tomb. Most tombs in Egypt are very inexpensive. This one I believe is now 100 Egyptian pounds, which is about 30 dollars, to get into. So that's a lot of money in Egypt. And it's the most expensive of all tombs. But it's worth it. And they're trying to keep down the number of people in it. When I last saw it, they were only selling about 100 tickets per day. Because any time you go into a tomb, you are perspiring and you are giving off water into the atmosphere. You are changing the humidity of the tomb. And that is, in a sense, leading to its destruction. So they have to control the number of people in this tomb. The Getty even suggested after they fixed it, after they restored it, that it be closed permanently. Interesting, just restoring it to have it for the heritage, but not for people to see. And I think eventually it may be closed. But it's a beautiful tomb. And Ramses built this for his beloved Nefertari.

Now that of course isn't the only one he's got to worry about. He's got 52 sons. What about Amunhirkepshef? What about Khaemwaset? Khaemwaset may have been buried in the north. We think he may have been buried in the Serapeum—we're not sure. But what about all these other sons? And this is where the famous KV5 comes in. The tomb in the Valley of the Kings, that has been numbered KV5. You know, as I mentioned once before, every tomb is numbered. And Kings Valley Five is the tomb that Ramses built for his sons. It was discovered really in the early part of the 19th century. Then it was lost—it was covered over. How did it get covered over? How does a tomb get covered over? There are occasional rainstorms in the Valley of the Kings. Infrequent. But when they come, boulders practically come rushing down through the Valley and rush into open tombs. So this tomb became blocked up, obliterated, and lost. It was rediscovered in 1987 by Kent Weeks, who is with the American University in Cairo. Weeks is in charge of a very important project, the Theban Mapping Project.

Believe it or not, there is no modern map of the Valley of the Kings. No modern map which accurately pinpoints and diagrams all the tombs. Kent Weeks has been doing this for 20 years, trying to do the most accurate map possible. It's an important project. And as part of his project—he knew that there was supposed to be this tomb, but he had to go find it. So he rediscovered it. In 1987. And they all got quite a shock when they went into it. They had to crawl in; the debris was so high that they had to crawl in on their bellies. They only had probably about three feet between the ceiling and the top of the debris. And they're crawling in. Two of them actually. The first was Kent Weeks. And another Egyptologist Catharine Roehrig. They crawled in, and they could see that there was a pillared hallway. And eventually they started clearing the tomb, because they had to diagram it. And that's when they got their shock—it's the largest tomb in all of Egypt. It has hundreds of rooms. Hundreds. And it's on several levels. I've been in the tomb. Only once. It's a little bit dangerous. It's not structurally sound. And you feel disoriented. It's not like any other tomb I've ever been in, because you've got all these rooms. And then you go down another level and you go back under, and there's more rooms. And the question is, what were all these rooms used for?

One possibility is, these are chapels where offerings could be made to the sons of Ramses. And then perhaps beneath will be the tombs of the sons. They have found objects that indicate this tomb was used for burials—pieces of coffins, pieces of the canopic jars, the jars that held the internal organs. This will be a very difficult excavation. Weeks has been working on it now for years. And you have to take out the debris. And it's like cement. And also—you can't just remove it all at once. You're going to change the humidity and the climate in the tomb, and walls are going to start moving. So this is an excavation that I think will probably take more than 100 years. They will probably have to clear one room, let the tomb stabilize, bring in the engineers to shore up the ceiling so it doesn't fall on you, and then maybe wait another 10 years. Excavate a little bit. So it's more than a lifetime project. But this is probably, it certainly, is the largest tomb in the Valley of the Kings. And Ramses built it for his sons.

Ramses also had to build his own tomb. Now with all these tombs being built, Ramses needed an entire city of workmen. And there is a city of the workmen called Deir el Medina, which is not far from the Valley of the Kings. And we know more about this city than any other ancient city in the world, because they left little notes to each other. We have potsherds with inscriptions on them. So we know how they constructed a tomb. We know that they had a right-hand gang. And a left-hand gang for Ramses's tomb. One [gang] would work on the right-hand wall. Others would work on the left-hand wall. And we even know things like—for example, their bronze chisels. They were weighed at the beginning of the week, and at the end of the week so nobody could steal any bronze. Because bronze was valuable. So you have your chisels. And they were weighed at the beginning at the end. Kind of like in the old days, when people used to shave the edges of gold coins to get a little bit when gold coins were in circulation. You'd shave the edge of maybe 1,000 coins. You'd have a little pile of gold. So they were weighed.

Now Ramses had an entire city working on these tombs. And Ramses's tomb, of course, is huge. It's terribly damaged, unfortunately. But it's huge. And my hunch is, that burial chamber of Ramses the Great probably held more treasure than any other room in the ancient world ever held. Think about Tutankhamen. Ten years to stuff it. Ramses had 67 years. So when Ramses died, he is buried in a major tomb. Now what I'd like to do next time is talk about, why did Ramses have this mid-life crisis? And the Exodus may have something to do with it. I'll see you then.

Lecture Thirty-Two
The Exodus—Did It Happen?

Scope:

The Book of Exodus is the section of the Old Testament most closely tied to Egypt and is fundamental to the history of the Jewish people, yet there is no direct archaeological evidence for its events. Here we examine the Egyptological record to see if such events could have occurred. We will discuss the difference between internal and external evidence and will even suggest who could have been the unnamed pharaoh of the Exodus—might it have been Ramses?

Outline

I. There is virtually no archaeological evidence for the Exodus. Nonetheless, the Exodus is the foundation of the Jewish faith in three parts and is mentioned more than any other event in the Old Testament. It presents the following stages of Israel's story: bondage, exodus, and coming to the Promised Land.

    A. The children of Israel are shown in bondage in the Bible.

        1. There was "a new pharaoh who knew not Joseph."

        2. The Bible says the Israelites worked in brick, not in stone. (Remember that these Israelites didn't build the pyramids, which date from much earlier.)

        3. Pharaoh tells the midwives to "watch the two stones" so they will kill the male Israelite children. We will see what that means shortly.

        4. Moses was born and named by the Egyptian princess because "I drew him out of the water." Nurtured by his mother, he matured, married, and encountered God in the form of the burning bush. God told Moses that the sons of Israel would be freed to find the Promised Land of milk and honey. Moses was given divine powers—his staff changed to a serpent.

        5. Moses had his audience with pharaoh ("the one who lives in the Great House"). No more straw for bricks will be given the Hebrews, pharaoh told him—they will have to gather it themselves.

        6. The 10 plagues descended: darkness (sandstorm), river of blood (topsoil), mosquitoes, and others. The first nine plagues, all possibly explained by natural phenomena, didn't move the pharaoh. But the tenth, the death of the first-born child, forced pharaoh to relent.

    7. Moses was told that Yahweh would harden the pharaoh's heart, but that in the end the Hebrews would plunder Egypt of silver and gold.

B. The Israelites left Egypt.

    1. As foreseen, they were given silver and gold.

    2. "600,000—all men—not counting families" were said to have left.

    3. They had been in Egypt for 430 years.

    4. They left not by the Philistine Road, but by the Sea of Reeds. (The "Red Sea" is a mistranslation.) The pharaoh pursued them.

    5. The Sea of Reeds parted, and the Israelites escaped. We are told of the Egyptians that "[Moses] clogged their chariot wheels." Were they actually stuck in the mud?

C. The Israelites wandered in the wilderness and eventually reached the Land of Canaan.

II. There are reasons why there is no external evidence for the Exodus.

A. The ancient Egyptians didn't record defeats; they had a different conception of history than we do.

B. Exodus was not an important event to the rest of the world (like the Middle East's reaction to the American Revolution). Maybe only a small number of the Israelites escaped—and their numbers were greatly exaggerated in the first place.

III. Internal evidence—consistency, accuracy of the depiction of Egypt—is how we have to make a judgment.

A. The cities of Pithom and Ramses are indeed real.

    1. They existed in the Delta, where the Israelites were.

    2. Bricks, not stone, were used for storehouses.

    3. Bricks with straw were not made in Canaan.

    4. Pharaoh's city was not called "Tanis" as it was in later times, when the Exodus was written.

B. Midwives told to watch "two stones," is probably a reference to Egyptian birthing stools, where women sat when giving birth.

C. "Pharaoh's heart was hardened," as the Bible puts it, was indeed an Egyptian concept.

D. The serpent "act" is also plausible—I found a snake charmer who could hold a cobra that stiffened like a walking stick.

E. Finally, the name "Moses" is pure Egyptian, meaning "birth."

IV. The external evidence is intriguing.

A. Ramses was probably the pharaoh of the Exodus.

1. Ramses built in the Delta, including a capital, Pi-Ramses.

2. Papyrus Leiden says, "distribute grain rations to the soldier and to the Apiru who transport stones to the great Pylon of Ramses." "Apiru" sounds like "Hebrew."

B. The Merneptah Stela (year 5—1207 B.C.), named for the 13th son of Ramses, helps place the Exodus in time.

1. "Canaan has been plundered into every sort of woe; Ashkelon has been overcome; Gezer has been captured. Yano'am was made nonexistent; Israel is laid waste, its seed is not." This is the earliest non-Biblical reference to Israel.

2. A determinative hieroglyph suggests that Israel is a people, not a place; they were still wandering when the stela was carved.

3. Counting backward, Exodus must have taken place during the reign of Ramses the Great (around year 20).

C. The death of Ramses's first-born child could have happened during Exodus.

V. So what *did* happen?

A. A handful of the children of Israel could have grown in the telling to 600,000 people.

B. A national history was written by Hebrew scholars for Hebrews, but there are kernels of truth the archaeologists still debate.

Essential Reading:

The Bible, Exodus 1–14.

Supplementary Reading:

Ernest S. Frerichs and Leonard H. Lesko, *Exodus, the Egyptian Evidence*.

Questions to Consider:

1. Is there any archaeological evidence for the Exodus?
2. Is there any internal evidence for the Exodus?

Lecture Thirty-Two—Transcript
The Exodus—Did It Happen?

Hello again. Welcome back. Remember last time, we ended with the death of my man Ramses the Great. I'd like to take a little bit of a chronological detour. And we're not going to talk about the next king. I want to talk about the Bible, about Exodus in particular. Because many people feel that Ramses is the pharaoh of the Exodus. Now what I'd like to do is, basically tell you the Exodus story. We'll talk about the story of Exodus as it is in the Bible. And then we'll look to see—how do you get evidence for this? Is there any internal evidence? Is there any external evidence? And we'll see. Did it really happen?

Now, first of all, about Exodus. One of the curious things about the Biblical tale of Exodus is that there is practically no archaeological evidence to support it. There are many things in the Bible that we have found archaeological evidence for. Many. But when it comes to Exodus, the record seems blank. There is no record of large numbers of Israelites in Egypt. We don't have a record of any man named Moses. None of that. So it's very difficult to try to figure out, did this thing really happen or not? But what we'll do is, as I say, we'll talk about the story as it's presented. And then we'll see, is there any way we can get some sort of evidence for it? Or maybe decide it didn't happen.

First the story. Well, one of the things about Exodus is it's the foundation of the Jewish faith. It is crucial. The Exodus story is mentioned more in the Old Testament than any other event in the Bible. It's mentioned more than any other event. And it really deals with three stages in the history of the Israelites. First, it's the Israelites in bondage. That's a part of it. Then it's the Exodus itself when they leave. And then it's the third stage, where they wander and finally come to the Promised Land. Let's start with Israel in bondage. Now remember, way back when we talked about the Joseph story? Joseph was the son of Jacob, called Israel. And this is why they're called the children of Israel. These are the 12 sons of Jacob, who eventually settle in Egypt. But this is way back in history for the Egyptians. But we know that there are these stories about Jacob's children, the children of Israel, being in Egypt. But when we left the story, remember, Joseph was the vizier of Egypt. He had saved Egypt because he figured out the dream—the pharaoh's dream. And he realized there would be seven good years, and seven years of famine. And by planning the economy for 14 years, by putting grain aside, he saves the economy. He's the hero. But that's in the past. Because the Exodus story starts with "and a new pharaoh came to the throne who knew not Joseph." So this is the past. And it's important. "He knew not Joseph." Meaning, this was the heyday of the Israelites in Egypt. This pharaoh didn't know about that.

Now, we are told many details in Exodus, and it's the details that makes it wonderful. For example, these Israelites who were now living in Egypt in the Delta area, they are numerous. They are prospering. And this bothers Pharaoh. He wants them to be under his thumb. So he puts taskmasters over them and enslaves them. Does all kinds of things to keep their numbers down, keep them in check. And the Bible says, they worked in brick. Now notice, by the way, they didn't work in stone. That's a detail. They're working in brick. That's important. Remember, by the way, these Israelites did not build the pyramids. The pyramids were built 1000 years earlier in the Old Kingdom. This is a common misconception often seen in movies. You know you've got these slaves, hauling blocks up. No way. Not only didn't they build the pyramids, they worked in brick. Now even so, they're becoming more numerous, these Israelites. And Pharaoh tells the midwives—and these were the people who were in charge of the births—tells the midwives, and it's a curious phrase. We'll talk about it later. But remember it. "Watch the two stones." That's what pharaoh says to the midwives. "Watch the two stones." Now what we'll do is, as an Egyptologist I'm going to try to interpret what this might mean. So we're going to go through the story first and then we'll see how it works. "Watch the two stones." So that they may kill the Israelite male children. Pharaoh wants the midwives to kill the male children. But they don't. They don't. They actually give Pharaoh a story when these male children keep popping up. And the pharaoh says, "hey, how come you didn't kill the male children? And they said, "Well, these Israelites are really tough. They give birth before we even get there." So they've got to—and we're even told by the way that the midwives are rewarded by Yahweh, by God, and they prosper because they did this thing.

Anyway we have Moses being born. A central thing. And his mother is of course afraid that he's going to be killed. A male Israelite. And then she sets him adrift in this basket. And the pharaoh's daughter finds the basket and she's going to take the kid in. And she names him "Moses." And the Bible tells us he's named Moses, because he is drawn out of the bulrushes. Taken out of the reeds. And the Hebrew word *moshe* is "to draw out." So that there's a kind of Hebrew etymology for this. It is kind of curious, by the way, that the pharaoh's daughter, this Egyptian woman, is going to name him a Hebrew name. Think about that. It's kind of curious. But anyway, that's what the Bible tells us. Moses is actually nurtured by his own mother. The princess has to get a wet nurse. So it's find some Israelite who will nurse him. And it's Moses's own mother who nurtures him. And he grows up. And eventually we know that he has an encounter with God in the burning bush. That's how he encounters God. And God, as the burning bush, tells Moses, he says, "Moses you're going to be instrumental in freeing the children of Israel from bondage." Now, Moses is a little hesitant. And he says, "Me? How am I going to do it?" And … it's kind of a personal interchange almost. He says, "How am I going to do this?" And God says, "Moses, don't worry. You've got a staff. Throw your staff down." And it turns into a snake. So Moses is going to be given these powers that will do it. And if you'll remember also, there's the thing with the hand. He never uses this. Moses's hand becomes leprous. He puts it in his cloak, it becomes leprous. He pulls it out, and it's healed. So the idea is, I'm behind you Moses. It will work. And Moses is instructed to go to Pharaoh and tell him, "Let my people go." And Moses says, I'm not really a good speaker. And that's basically what he says. I don't really speak that well. How can I do this? And God says, all right. You can take Aaron with you. Your brother, who's a better speaker. Moses said, "I'm slow of speech." So the deal is, that Moses can take Aaron.

He's going with divine powers. He's going to go to Pharaoh, and tell Pharaoh, "Let my people go." He has the audience with Pharaoh. Now, crucial for us—we are never told who the pharaoh is. The only way he is referred to is as "pharaoh." Now "Pharaoh" up until this point is not an Egyptian way of referring to the king. It's not really. *Nesu* was one way the king was called, there are many words for king. Pharaoh is not quite the normal way—it's a corruption. Or a conjunction, actually, of two Egyptian words. *Per,* which means "house," and *a,h* which means "great." So it's a person who lived in the Great House, the palace, the king. So he is referred to as "the one who lives in the Great House." The *per-ah*, the pharaoh. This is when we first get this term introduced. Later in Egyptian history, we'll even get it used on temple walls, *per-ah*, but no. This is an unusual term.

So he's referred to only as "pharaoh." We don't know who he is. We don't. The only clue we get to his identity, is that the cities that the Israelites are building with these bricks are called the cities of "Ramses" and "Pitum." So one of the cities is named Ramses. But remember, there are plenty of kings named Ramses. And Pitum means something like "the house of Atum." So it's a "god city." And they're building these "store cities," we're even told. Store cities, that means, where you store things. So we don't know who pharaoh is, but they go to him and they say, "Hey, let my people go." Not only that—I mean, it's what we would call *chutzpah*—they say, we want three days off to celebrate a festival to our God. It's amazing. And Pharaoh really thinks this is outrageous. And Moses does the serpent thing. He knows he's got this staff that God showed him, and he throws the staff down. You know, it's actually Aaron's staff that's thrown on the ground. And it turns into a serpent.

But the amazing thing when you read the Bible—and everybody that's your homework assignment, Exodus 1 through 14. You'll love it after this I think. Exodus 1 through 14. The amazing thing in this story is nobody's impressed! Pharaoh's magicians take their staffs. They throw them down. And they turn into serpents. Apparently, it's the old snake trick that everybody knew. Only then, the only saving thing for Moses, is that his staff swallows the others. So that's pretty good, it's a plus. At least he's won. And it's an interesting thing about how nobody's impressed by this staff turning into a serpent. But anyway, Pharaoh refuses.

He says, not only that, you're not getting your three days off to celebrate your holiday. And we are not going to give you any straw for your bricks. Now this is crucial. Bricks in Egypt were made with straw to give them strength. You chopped straw and mixed it in with the clay, so that your bricks would have a kind of consistency that would hold together. It was for strength. Now in the 19th century, by the way, there were quasi-Biblical scholars who were looking throughout Egypt for bricks without straw, as evidence of the Bible. But this was kind of silly, really. If you read the text carefully, they're not telling the Israelites to make bricks without straw. They're telling the Israelites, you've got a quota. You've got to make the same number of bricks. But now we're not going to supply the chopped straw. You're going to have to chop your own straw, mix it into the mud, and make it into bricks. That's what you're going to have to do. So it's harder work. You've got the same quota. More jobs to do. Because you've got to chop your straw and all that. So it's just more difficult.

And by the way, as part of my sort of research on the Exodus, I went to brickyards in ancient Egypt in the south. And they still make bricks the same way. They use cut tires. Cut truck tires as baskets. And they have chopped straw. They dump it in. They mix it in the mud with their feet. And then they have little brick molds. And they make bricks. It's quite interesting to see. It's back into Biblical times.

Anyway, the pharaoh refuses. He's not going to let them go. You've got to make more. More work for you. And then come the plagues, as you all know, the 10 plagues. And the first nine plagues do not convince Pharaoh to let the Israelites go. We have darkness. The river turns to blood. We have mosquitoes. We have boils. We have frogs. We have locusts. All these plagues. Now the interesting thing to me about the first nine plagues is, that they can all be explained as natural phenomena. Even the river turning to blood. Remember, when we talked about the inundation, when the Nile overflowed its banks? And what happened was that from the south you get these monsoon rains from Ethiopia, swelling the Nile. And with it comes topsoil. Red topsoil. So the river actually did turn red once a year. So that's not that astounding. You know, when you call it blood, it might be blood red. Or even for example darkness. One of the plagues is when darkness comes during the day. Sand storm perhaps. Mosquitoes. Boils. You know it's all natural phenomena.

But the one plague that seems to really be different, the one that eventually moves Pharaoh, is the death of the firstborn. Moses tells Pharaoh all the firstborn children will be killed. Now Moses has been told by God that his people will be spared. If you'll remember the story, he is told to take the blood of a lamb, and they put it over the doorsill of the Israelites' houses. So that the Angel of Death, when he comes to slay all the firstborn—and it's firstborn cattle, it's firstborn of the maid who is working on the grindstone—the Angel of the Lord will see the blood and will pass over that household. And that's why today of course we have the celebration called Passover. It celebrates the passing over of the Angel of the Lord so that the firstborn of the Israelites were spared. And of course it happens. All the firstborn are killed. And this is when Pharaoh finally relents, when he finally says you can go. And this is when the Exodus begins.

Now there's a funny detail. I'm not sure exactly what it means. But when Moses was talking to God in the form of the burning bush, God said, "You'll be freed." God even says, Yahweh says to Moses, "Pharaoh's heart will be hardened." But he even says that he, Yahweh, will harden Pharaoh's heart. So there seems to be some sort of test of the Israelites' resolve. But he says, "When you leave, you will leave with gold and silver. You will plunder the Egyptians." So that's what God says, and that's what happens. Everybody is so shocked by this death of the firstborn that when the Israelites want to take gold and silver, they give it to them. So the Israelites start to leave on their Exodus with gold and silver.

Now, how many are involved in the Exodus? The Bible tells us 600,000. And it even says men, not including families. The Hebrew is *elfeim*. You know, 1,000. It's a plural of "thousand." Six hundred thousand men, not including families. Now that's a large number. The population of Egypt probably was about a million at the time. So it's a kind of number that you use to say, "whoa, something is wrong here." But that's what we're told. And the Bible says they had been in Egypt for 430 years. So we have an idea of the time since Joseph perhaps.

Now how do they leave? Well obviously, they're leaving on foot. And we are told some details of their route. First, they don't leave by the "Philistine route." Now the Philistine route is going into Palestine. You know we get Palestine from Philistine. And this is a route that's guarded; there are watchtowers. They don't want to go that route. So they go through—they're in the Delta—they go through the marsh. Now there is a common mistranslation of *yam suf*, which is the word for where they go through. It's the "Sea of Reeds." They don't go through the Red Sea. No. They're not swimming, or whatever. It's the Sea of Reeds. And we're even given a detail I think, that suggests why it's the Sea of Reeds that makes much more sense. As they're escaping, if you remember, God parts the waters. People are afraid, but God parts the waters. And then if you'll remember, Pharaoh all of a sudden changes his mind, jumps into his chariot, takes some of his charioteers, and they pursue the

Israelites. And we're told that the chariots of Pharaoh are "clogged." Now that sounds like they're going through mud. See, the Israelites undoubtedly don't have chariots. They weren't used to that kind of thing, they were the slaves. They're going on foot. They're dragging whatever they can. But chariots could get bogged down in the Sea of Reeds, where people could indeed walk through it. So in the end we know the river is closed on Pharaoh's army. And they perish.

And then comes the wandering of course. They wander in the wilderness and eventually reach the Promised Land of milk and honey. The Exodus story. Now, let's see if we can get any evidence for it. Is there any way you could try to—because as I say, there's no straightforward archaeological evidence? No man named Moses. No large list of Israelite captives. None of that. Well, first of all, why is there no record of it if it happened? Well, I think one reason is the Egyptian concept of history. They never kept records of defeat. Never. They never recorded losses, and this would have been a loss. If you read all of the battle accounts of all the pharaohs, they won every one. They just—some of them they kept winning closer to home, as they retreated. But there's no sense of objective history. So the Egyptians wouldn't have recorded it.

Another reason, perhaps, why we don't get a record of it is—this is crucial to the Israelites. It is a foundation of their religious faith. But it wasn't that important to anyone else in the Middle East. It was an event that happened perhaps to a small number of people. Now if I had to guess—now I've already said, I think 600,000 is certainly impossible.

But you know how stories are, when you tell it. The fish gets bigger. And the victory gets bigger. So in the course of telling the story, it grows to thousands. My bet is, something happened. Six hundred maybe. It could even be maybe 60. Maybe it's a couple of large families that get out. But I think it's the kind of event that the Middle East, the ancient Middle East, just didn't care about. You think the Hittite king cares about what's happening, there are these people leaving? It's a little bit like, look in the Middle East's records in the 1770s for what's happening in America. The American Revolution. There's not much about it. Nobody cared. And it may be a similar thing. So it's not surprising that we don't have records. But do we have any way of getting at this thing? Is it true? Is it false? Let's look at internal evidence.

Does the story hold together internally? Well first of all, there were indeed cities of Pithom and Ramses. Those are talked about in the Bible. They existed in the Delta. Just where the Israelites worked. Ramses built them. Now bricks are used for storehouses. Not stone. That's good, that works. Also, bricks are made with straw. In Egypt they are. But you know in Canaan, they didn't make bricks with straw. So this is a nice detail, where the Canaanites writing this story later are saying they've got it right. The Egyptians used straw. That's pretty good. Also, the names of the towns are pretty good. You know when it says Pithom and Ramses. They could have been using later names. In the Bible they could have used Tanis, which it was called later. People thought it was that. No. They don't. They've got the names right. That's pretty good. Also you know what I think about sometimes—remember Aaron and Moses are coming daily to Pharaoh. "Ah, you didn't like boils, wait until you see locusts." They keep coming back and forth. Well they were working in the Delta, right next to the palace. So that makes it possible to go back and forth. And they have these conferences with the pharaoh daily. So the logistics sort of works.

Now remember the midwives. I said, remember that thing about "watch the two stones." That's a nice detail. Ancient Egyptian women gave birth in a seated position. It's a good position to give birth in—gravity helps you. Gravity assists the birth. And women used a special birthing stool which was sometimes two blocks of stone. And you sat on the two blocks of stone. Or sometimes it was built up out of bricks. So when the midwives are told, "watch the two stones," that's good Egyptian detail. Somebody knew what he was talking about. These people were in Egypt. This is a good detail. So there is some kind of internal consistency here.

Also you know that phrase; "Pharaoh's heart was hardened." Very Egyptian. Very Egyptian. The Egyptians believed you thought with your heart. Because when you get excited of course it's your heart that beats quickly, not your brain. And the heart was viewed as the seat of all emotions. So Pharaoh's heart was hardened. That's a nice detail. I like that.

Now I think one of the things that I sort of liked—the serpent trick. The old serpent trick. I wondered about that. I've wondered about that for years. And about five years ago, I was in Egypt. And I decided to see if I could find a snake charmer. There are still snake charmers in Egypt. It's a wonderful thing. I wanted to see if I could find a snake charmer who could do it. You know, I figured, if Pharaoh's men aren't impressed it's got to be a trick that people knew. I found a snake charmer in the south of Egypt who worked with cobras. Now I don't know if these were poisonous or not, if they had been de-fanged, or what. But they were cobras. There's no question about that. And I said, hey can you do this? Can you make your cobra look like a staff? And he did it. It was not exactly as in the Bible, but I was impressed. He took this cobra. And he holds it up in his hand. And this cobra is kind of wriggling around. Kind of wriggling a lot. And all of a sudden, the cobra goes rigid. And it looks like the top of the cobra's head is the top of a walking stick. And you've got this guy holding what looks like a staff, with the head carved like a cobra. And then he throws it on the ground. And it wriggles away. That's pretty good. I mean sure it's pressure on nerves. He's probably squeezing the poor thing to death. Who knows what. But this cobra looked like a staff.

Then he did something that really blew me away. I hadn't asked. I didn't know what was coming. And he kind of had this standard magic trick I guess he did. He took the cobra and he tied it in a knot. And he put it on top of his head, so that you had the cobra's head kind of pointing out towards you from him. And you know what it looked like? Remember that the sign of the pharaoh was the *uraeus*, the cobra on the forehead? That's what it looked like. And I mean he had no idea that this went back to ancient Egypt. But it certainly looked like that, that he had a crown with a cobra coming out of it. So even this serpent trick, there's still some traces of it in Egypt.

Now what about his name—Moses. Remember I said we'd talk about Moses. It is not reasonable to think that a princess, an Egyptian princess, is going to pick a kid out of the water and then start speaking Hebrew and give him an Egyptian name. Moses. No. That's a bad etymology. It doesn't work. Moses is a purely Egyptian name. It means birth. And it makes sense given that she's got this kid now. A new kid. It's like her birth. She calls him Moses. Moses is pure Egyptian. For example Ramses's name is really Ra-Meses—"Ra is born." The pharaoh Tuthmosis III, our great warrior. It means Toth, the ibis headed god, is born. So this is a purely Egyptian name. And it makes more sense when you look at it from an Egyptological standpoint, than just biblical, that oh, it's a Hebrew word. No. So that's pretty good too. Now that's a lot of internal stuff.

What about external stuff? You know, is there any way we could find evidence for the Exodus? Well, as I said, the Delta is pretty good. Ramses's capital—Ramses the Great, and I'm going to suggest that he might be the pharaoh of the Exodus. They did build a city of Ramses, and Pithom. His capital was in the Delta. He built these big cities. So it's starting to look like there's some bit of historicity to this story. Also, let me tell you about a papyrus that's in the Leiden Museum. It's got just one sentence that's important, but it's a really good sentence for us. Here's what it says. It's instructions for workers, for overseers of workers. And it says "distribute grain rations to the soldiers and to the Apiru, to transport stones to the great Pylon of Ramses." Now Ramses's city was being built also, not just the store city. You had temples. And it says "soldiers and Apiru." Sounds very much like Hebrew. And many people think that the *hapiru*, who were a Bedouin [tribe] in the north, that these may be the Hebrews. So we have a suggestion that this may be our Israelites. Maybe in Egypt.

Now there's one more bit that's really the cornerstone. It's called the "Merneptah Stela." Now remember Ramses's firstborn son, Amunhirkepshef. He died before he became pharaoh. It's the 13th son. And we're going to talk a lot about him next time. He's the 13th son, Merneptah, who becomes king. In the fifth year of his reign, he erects the stela talking about all of his victories. This is the first time in the Egyptian record where Israel is mentioned. We never get it during the reign of Ramses. We get it during the fifth year of the reign of Merneptah. And I'll tell you what he says on this stela. He says "Canaan has been plundered into every sort of woe." So he's going to list the countries that he's beaten up. "Canaan has been plundered into every sort of woe. Ashkelon has been overcome. Gezer has been captured. Yano'am has been made a non-existent. Israel is laid waste. Its seed is not." Israel is laid waste. Its seed is not. The first mention of Israel. Important to note, he's not talking about the Exodus. Many people think Merneptah is the pharaoh of the Exodus. But he's talking about battles outside of Egypt. He's listing all these places he's beaten up.

But what's crucial is this—it's the way the word "Israel" is written. If you look at all of these countries that he's talking about. He's got Canaan, Ashkelon, Gezer. All of these at the end of that word for that country is the sign for a foreign land. It's a hill. Three hills. Because foreign lands had lots of hills. That's how you said "country." When he refers to Israel, there is no country sign. What you have is a sign of a man and a woman. In other words, Israel at this point is not a country. It's not an established place. It's a people. Now what that suggests, is that they have not established themselves yet; they are still wandering. So during the time of Merneptah, it suggests that Israel has not yet established itself.

Now if you do a little mathematics, which is kind of neat, if you count backwards, year five of Merneptah the only pharaoh whose reign this could have come into with the Israelites as still wandering is the previous one, Ramses the Great, who ruled for 67 years. And many people, biblical scholars—Kenneth Kitchen is a great scholar on Ramses the Great—suggest that it happened some time around year 20 of Ramses's reign even. Some time around there. Now what's interesting is that—remember that's when Ramses's firstborn son Amunhirkepshef dies—roughly. Roughly. So we've got some consistency here, that something may have happened. May have. The death of Ramses's firstborn child may indeed have come during this Exodus period, and Amunhirkepshef may be that firstborn son who dies. So it is possible. It is possible that something happened. Not 600,000 people. Something much smaller. But there is some evidence that something like the Exodus may have happened. And if it did, I think it probably happened during the reign of Ramses the Great.

But next time, we'll talk a little bit more about Ramses, but a different Ramses. We're going to talk about Ramses's mummy, and then about this 13th son, Merneptah, who becomes king of Egypt. We'll do that next.

Lecture Thirty-Three
The Decline of Dynasty XIX

Scope:

Here we will see Egypt begin a long slide from greatness that will finally end 1,200 years later with the death of Egyptian civilization. One indication of decline is the short reigns; another, the absence of major building projects.

Outline

I. The mummy of Ramses revealed a great deal about his last years.

    A. Discovered in the Deir el Bahri cache, it remained in Cairo for a century, rehydrating and growing fungi. No one ever thought a mummy needed conservation like other objects. It is the only pharaoh's mummy ever to leave Egypt.

    B. Taken to Paris (in 1976) for treatment, Ramses had 89 species of fungi growing on him. Gamma-ray irradiation was used to kill the growths; we're not sure whether the DNA was affected.

    C. Placed in a case of nitrogen "azote" made by the Getty Conservation Institute, Ramses was now fully sterilized and given a clean bill of health before being returned to Cairo.

    D. Ramses also had arteriosclerosis, not to mention a hole in his mandible from an infection that may have killed him. X-rays show Ramses's heart on the wrong side, sewn in with gold thread. Perhaps the embalmers made a mistake and repaired it with gold "eternal" thread.

    E. Ramses's red hair may have had religious significance, because the followers of Seth were said to be red-headed.

II. Merneptah, "the beloved of Ptah," ruled from 1212–1202 B.C.

    A. The 13th son of Ramses, he must have been 60 when he became king.

    B. His famous Victory Stela (year 5) was found by Petrie at his mortuary temple at Thebes. It describes his Canaanite campaign: "Israel is devastated, its seed is no more." For a long time, some thought he was the pharaoh of the Exodus.

C. One of his inscriptions on Karnak Temple tells of "the uncircumcised phalli of 6,359 Libyans killed [and] carried off." Because the Egyptians were circumcised, they cut the penises off the enemy corpses as proof of a body count. Although traditionally the Egyptians cut off enemy hands, perhaps they used a different tack this time to avoid the accusation that they killed women.

D. Merneptah built a palace at Memphis, now mostly lost because of the high water table.

E. His tomb in the Valley of the Kings is one of the most interesting. In 1920, Howard Carter discovered 13 large alabaster jars near the tomb; the inscriptions on the jars indicated that they had held the sacred oils used in the mummification of Merneptah.

F. Merneptah was buried in three nested sarcophagi of pink Aswan granite. The sarcophagi and walls of his tomb were decorated with religious texts from "The Book of Gates."

III. Amenmesses, son of Merneptah (1202–1199 B.C.), is a mystery king. He was not the crown prince but became pharaoh. The son of a minor wife, Takhat, he built a tomb in the Valley of the Kings (KV 10).

IV. Seti II (1199–1193 B.C.) succeeded Amenmesses and erased his name, a common practice in ancient Egypt. The worst fate that could befall a pharaoh was to be ignored by history—it was also a convenient way to take credit for other pharaohs' work.

A. He had three queens, or wives. Tiaa was the mother of Siptah, the next king. Twosret would later actually rule Egypt.

B. Seti II built a boat shrine at Karnak for the sacred barques of Amun, Mut, and Khonsu.

V. The mummy of Siptah (1193–1187 B.C.), the son of Seti II, was found in the Deir el Bahri cache. He had a deformed foot, possibly from polio.

VI. Twosret (1187–1185 B.C.), the stepmother of Siptah, ruled as king, a sign of turmoil in Egypt.

A. She had a small tomb (KV 14) for herself in the Valley of the Kings.

B. She had a separate small burial for jewelry that was discovered in 1908. One level contained a considerable amount of gold leaf, but most impressive was a necklace and pair of silver gloves containing eight finger rings.

Essential Reading:

Peter Clayton, *Chronicle of the Pharaohs*, pp. 156–159.

Supplementary Reading:

Aidan Dodson, *Monarchs of the Nile*, Chapter XII.

Questions to Consider:

1. Why is Merneptah considered by some to be the pharaoh of the Exodus?

2. What indications are there of Egypt's eventual decline?

Lecture Thirty-Three—Transcript
The Decline of Dynasty XIX

Hi. Welcome back. Remember last time we talked about the Exodus, and how possibly, just possibly, Ramses might be the pharaoh of the Exodus. He's the greatest king of the XIXth Dynasty. But after his reign, Egypt sort of starts to slide and go downhill. And I want to talk about that slide. But I'd like to also talk about—I don't want to leave you without telling you about Ramses's mummy. It's a great story. I want to tell you about the mummy of Ramses the Great. Because it maybe gives us a clue as to why Egypt started its long slide. The mummy was found in the famous cache of royal mummies at Deir el Bahri that we talked about, when the priest kings had gathered together mummies for safety, because there were robberies in the Valley of the Kings. Ramses is one of those mummies that was put away in a secret tomb and remained undisturbed for 3,000 years.

Now the mummy tells a great story. First, after the mummy was discovered, it was brought to Cairo to be placed in a museum. And it's now in the Egyptian Museum. You can actually see the mummy of Ramses the Great. It may be the only face you ever look on of a Biblical figure. I mean, think about it—how many actual faces from the Bible can you see? But Ramses's mummy remained in the Egyptian Museum for about a century almost. Untouched practically, and that was the problem. The mummy was viewed as a dead person, rather than a museum object. So there was no conservation done on it. And in the humid atmosphere of Cairo it was starting to grow fungi, and it was starting to decay. You could actually see 19th-century photos of Ramses and 20th-century photos of Ramses. And you could see the decay. So something had to be done.

Now the mummy of Ramses the Great is the only pharaoh's mummy ever to leave Egypt. It was decided that Ramses had to be refurbished—saved. So the mummy was flown to France. It was going to be worked on at the Museum of Man by a team of scientists to see what they could do about stopping the fungi, reversing the damage, and fixing Ramses. An interesting story by the way. How do you get the mummy of a king through customs? What do you label him as? When he touched down, when the plane touched down in Paris, he was given the full treatment of a head of state—of a visiting head of state. The band was there, because he was a king of

Egypt. So he was given the full treatment, Ramses, and taken to the museum.

And then the study began. They had to be very gentle with Ramses. I mean, it is a three-thousand-year-old mummy. And so gentle for example—he was flown in the coffin that he had been in. It was a modern coffin that they made for him on display. But they didn't want to lift him up even. So they cut the end of the coffin and slid him out rather than lifting it. They were just afraid to really do almost anything to him.

So they studied him. And they found 89 different species of fungi on Ramses. I mean they had to kill these fungi. The problem is, of course, how do you do that without damaging the mummy itself? You can't heat it—you might normally try to heat it. You can't even freeze it because it would contract, and perhaps that would cause damage. What do you do? They finally hit on a solution that has been used in operating rooms for years—gamma ray sterilization. Very often, by the way, surgical tools are gamma-ray irradiated. That's how you sterilize them. You nuke them, basically, and they're perfectly sterile. And this doesn't cause changes. Has that great advantage. So they nuked Ramses. They irradiated him with gamma rays. But before they did that, they took pieces of unimportant mummies and tested them to see if there was any change in the color of the skin, for example. They even used some parchment as a test. So Ramses was irradiated. And that was good; that worked just fine. In the future, by the way, there may be a problem with that, just maybe. This was before anybody ever thought about doing DNA studies on mummies. And we don't know what gamma-ray irradiation has done to the DNA of Ramses the Great, whether we'll be able to recover it now in future studies. But at least the fungi were killed, and Ramses was sterile.

Now how do you keep Ramses sterile? Well, the Getty Museum helps here. Now remember the Getty Institute is the one that restored the tomb of Nefertari, Ramses's wife. So it's kind of nice that they had a part in restoring Ramses the Great. They designed a case. They wanted a case that was simple. Very simple. That you could keep him. Low maintenance. That could be maintained in Cairo quite easily. And they came upon this solution of nitrogen. Let me explain. When the components of air were first discovered—remember the old chemist, Levoisier and the French figuring out what the parts of air were. They called nitrogen "azote." Now the French word *azote* means "without life." "Azote," without life. And they called nitrogen "azote" because when they did experiments and put little animals like mice in nitrogen, they died. Because there's no oxygen. So nothing could live in an atmosphere of nitrogen. So they designed a case, a plexiglas case. With an atmosphere of nitrogen in it, and Ramses was put inside that case. So that now nothing is going to grow in that case. He's virtually sterile.

The shipment back, by the way, was really quite interesting. Because you didn't want to open the case and then let things in. You want nitrogen. And they shipped the case in a kind of almost—like these bubbles that you put children without immune systems in. And they had tools and everything. So it was to install Ramses in his coffin in the Egyptian Museum in Cairo. So he's there. And he's, as we say, dead and well. The mummy has been refurbished, re-wrapped; it's doing fine. But let me tell you about what we learned about Ramses from the mummy itself. It's a different picture from what you get when you read the temple inscriptions that Ramses left us. There's a tendency to think always of Ramses as this youthful guy riding off into battle. He's got all these wives, he's got 100 kids, everything is fine on the Nile. Ramses died a cripple probably.

Now remember, he ruled for 67 years. He is probably about 88 years old when he dies. That's quite an age in Egypt. He is the second-longest reigning monarch in Egypt. Think back to the Old Kingdom. Remember the end of the Old Kingdom? The Old Kingdom ended with Pepi II, a pharaoh who reigned for 94 years. The longest-reigning monarch in the history of the world. Ruled for 94 years. He was a child of course when he took over. But remember we talked about that that may have been the reason why Egypt went downhill. The pharaoh was supposed to be the physical leader of the country. He wasn't like the Prime Minister or the President. He had to physically lead the army. So maybe Egypt went downhill under Pepi II because he couldn't maintain the army anymore. He wasn't looking after business. The same thing may have happened with Ramses. In his late 80s when he dies, he certainly didn't ride out anymore. Maybe he couldn't even take care of business. So possibly the age of Ramses may have contributed to this decline that we're going to see today in the XIXth Dynasty.

But there's some other great things about the mummy of Ramses. I mean, one thing for example, we know he suffered from arteriosclerosis. The x-rays of Ramses show that the arteries are clogged. The femoral arteries, as a matter of fact, are clogged. He also had a terrible infection in the mandible. Terrible. Massive. He may have even died from it. Remember, the Egyptians had no way of treating infection. They had no germ theory. They had no idea of what was causing this. And Ramses's mandible shows a tremendous infection. It was common for Egyptians to suffer tooth decay. But not because of what our common—our causes, like sugar. No. They didn't have a lot of sugar in their diet. The wealthy maybe had honey. What caused the decay was their bread. Commoners and kings ate the same kind of bread. Basically it was stone-ground. And as the bread was stone-ground you get a little bit of the stone in your grain. Not only that, if you've got a desert country, sand is blowing into it. So when you bake your bread, it's got quite a bit of grit in it. And as you chew it, you're literally sanding down your teeth. Almost all the mummies I examine, even young ones, have teeth that are worn down from chewing this bread. Now what that does is it exposes the pulp of the tooth. And that's when you get your decay. So it's not because of sugar, or honey, or whatever, it's because of these ground-down teeth. And that may have really ultimately done in Ramses the Great.

There's a real interesting feature to Ramses. I mean I love the mummy of Ramses the Great; it's a great mummy. The first really neat thing is, the heart's in the wrong place. I don't mean that figuratively, you know, that Ramses had his heart in the wrong place, he's a bad guy, it's in the wrong place. It's on the wrong side of the body. Let me explain. At mummification, the heart was left in the body. Because as you know, the Egyptians believed you thought with your heart. So when you're resurrected, you'd need it to think, say the magical spells, etcetera. So the heart was left in the body. Now when Ramses was x-rayed, it looks as if his heart—I mean, there's no question about it, the heart was on the wrong side of the body—but it looks as if the heart is sewn into place with perhaps gold thread. Now the only thing I can think of that could have caused that, is maybe when the embalmers—working on the mummy of the king, removed the internal organs took out the stomach, liver, intestines, and lungs—go in through the diaphragm in to the thoracic. You have two cavities, abdominal below the thoracic. Go into the thoracic—they're taking out the lungs. And perhaps they damaged the heart. Perhaps they cut it. And perhaps, just perhaps, the heart falls out by mistake. Well then, they've got to put it back in, and this would have been a really difficult thing. Suturing up Ramses internally with gold thread. Now, you'd use gold thread because gold never tarnishes. That's the metal of eternity. Even the burial chamber of a pharaoh was called the "Gold Room." So you would use gold thread because it would last forever. So it seems as if the mummy of Ramses may have had some really interesting repairs on it in ancient times.

Another interesting feature of my man Ramses is that he was a redhead. We can tell that from analysis of his hair. It's not that as you get older, of course, your hair changes color. But Ramses really had natural red hair. Now this may have a religious significance. Remember Ramses's father was Seti I. And Seti was an unusual name, because it showed an allegiance to the god Seth. Not one of the dominant gods. Well, the followers of Seth were always said to have red hair. And maybe Ramses's whole family were redheads that some how had this following for the god Seth, and that's why they were sort of associated with Seth. It's an interesting thing, but he was red-headed.

But Ramses today lies in the Egyptian Museum, in the mummy room. And you can see him today—the pharaoh who went out to Kush and did battle. He's there. It's real history. But as I say, perhaps Ramses's range is too long, because Egypt is going to slip during the XIXth Dynasty. And that's what I want to talk about now. This slipping, this slow decline. Now remember Ramses had all these sons. Probably 52 of them I think is the number that's used now. Well naturally, many of them are going to pre-decease him. They're going to die before Ramses. Ramses was proud of his kids. On the wall at Luxor Temple, for example, you can see a procession of his children. The sons are lined up. And they've got their names under them. Right on the front. You can see Amunhirkepshef, the firstborn, and you count a few more down, you'll see Khaemwaset—that archaeologist kid, who did the excavations. And then, if you count down 13 you'll see Merneptah. The 13th son, who becomes king of Egypt. And what that means is of course, that the first 12 died before Ramses. So we get this 13th son, Merneptah, being king of Egypt.

Now, don't think of him as a kid. He's probably 60 years old by the time he ascends the throne. His name is nice. It means it means "the beloved of Ptah." "Mer" is the word for "love." And "beloved." Mer. And the "N." means "of" and Ptah, the god Ptah. So he's the beloved of Ptah. It's a nice name. And he's the one who erects the famous Victory Stela. In the fifth year of his reign, he erects that round-top stone talking about his victories in the area of Canaan. And he's the one who says, "Israel is destroyed. Its seed is no longer." And for a long time, many people said that Merneptah was the pharaoh of the Exodus, just because he is the first one to mention Israel. But remember what I said last time. It is clear from this inscription that he's not talking about the Exodus. He is talking about defeating a group of different countries and peoples outside the borders of Egypt. So Merneptah is not the pharaoh of the Exodus. I'm really quite sure of it. Now he does do battle, of course. I mean he has this Victory Stela. And he says he loves to beat up people. I mean he likes that.

He talks about fighting the Libyans. Now the Libyans are to the west, and they will become a threat later. And as a matter of fact in a couple of hundred years, you're going to see Libyans ruling Egypt. But now they're not any real power, not a real force to be reckoned with. But remember to get from Libya to Egypt, to invade Egypt, is a big deal. You're going across a desert, and you can get lost. So it was a big deal to fight the Libyans. And he fights the Libyans, and he defeats them. And Mereptah on a wall at Karnak Temple talks about this defeat.

And there's an amazing inscription. I'm one of the few people who brings his students to see this inscription. Many of the Egyptian guides—they're very genteel, and they don't want to show it. Let me explain it. I'll tell you what it says first. It says, "the uncircumcised penises of 6,359 Libyans killed were carried off." Now what does that mean? The ancient Egyptians in a battle had army scribes, guys whose job it was to keep track of how many you kill, how many you capture, all that. Now a battle, of course, takes place on a large field. And imagine it. There's confusion. You have hand-to-hand battle it's not at a distance. And at the end of the battle—Egypt, of course, has won—and you've got this field that's strewn with bodies.

How do you count the number? It's not easy. I mean one scribe walking all over the field—One, two, three? Or do you have five scribes calling, and you hope they don't count the same guy? Well, to make it easier the tradition in Egypt was to cut off a hand. They would hack off a hand. Bring it to a central place on the battlefield. Pile them up. And the scribes would count the hands. That's how you kept track of how many you had killed. Now sometimes, if you wanted a big display of your valor and victory, you bring the hands back. You can bring the hands back. And you have cartloads of hands. I mean, rather gruesome. But that was the idea, you're going to show I'm powerful. I'm brutal. Don't mess with me. Now somebody may have said—we don't know exactly why the penises are cut off in this particular battle. Somebody may have said, if you bring back the hands, how do we know these aren't the hands of women? How do we know they're the hands of men? Merneptah answered that question. He brought back the penises. And notice the inscription says uncircumcised. That's a kind of derogatory thing. The Egyptians considered themselves superior; they were circumcised. The Egyptians practiced circumcision. It was done when a boy reached puberty. Not at birth. And this was a real sign of being Egyptian. And even—you know, last time we were talking about the Exodus—where did the Jews get the idea of circumcision? It could have been from the Egyptians. So Merneptah is proud of this battle with the Libyans where he brings back penises, uncircumcised ones.

He also builds. He has a palace that he builds, in the Delta area, at Memphis, the capital of Egypt. But it's gone. It's terribly damaged. And the reason is—the Delta was a marshy area. Memphis is not in the Delta, but it's near enough that the water table is high. So the palaces sunk underground. And all we have are a few blocks now, but it was undoubtedly a great palace. He was a builder like his father Ramses the Great. His tomb is interesting also. Howard Carter, the discoverer of Tutankhamen's tomb, made an interesting discovery right outside Merneptah's tomb. In a pit, he found 13 large alabaster jars. By large, I mean they're probably two feet high, maybe three feet high. And technically they're not alabaster by the way—calcite. Egypt doesn't have true alabaster. It looks pretty good to me, and when it's sold to tourists it's always called alabaster. But it's really calcite. But these are large jars. And they were used in the mummification of Merneptah, before they put the body in the tomb. And they were considered sacred because they were part of the mummification. So they were buried near the tomb. Interesting discovery; 1920. Howard Carter did that.

But the tomb is interesting. Merneptah was buried in a fantastic sarcophagus. Fantastic. It was actually three nested sarcophagi, one inside the other. Really quite an impressive thing. I mean they were massive, massive things to protect the body forever. And on his tomb walls was the Book of Gates. It's a magical text that's going to enable the pharaoh to get to the next world. On the journey to the next world, you're going to have to go through gates. Think about it—an Egyptian temple. You always had to go through a pylon, a gateway. And the idea was, the next world is going to be the same. And it's going to be pretty impressive. Not only that though, there's going to be people who want to keep you out of the gates. There will be gatekeepers. And you had to know the names of the gatekeepers, and what was going to happen. It was the secret words. And on the walls of the tomb of Merneptah we have the Book of the Gates. So his tomb is in a sense not only going to protect the body of Merneptah, it's going to help him get to the next world.

Now after Merneptah, after the death of Merneptah, we have a strange, strange decline. It's a curious period in the dynasty. Why? Well, let's think of what's happened. Ramses the Great ruled for 67 years. Sixty-seven years. Maybe too long. Maybe he can't really lead the army. Maybe the army isn't maintained. But now we get his son. Oh, but his son is 60 years old when he gets on the throne. So we've got this problem of older pharaohs. And Egypt almost always goes downhill when the pharaoh lives too long. So what happens after Merneptah? We get a mystery king—Amenmesses. Rules for about two years. Now why do I call him a mystery king? He wasn't supposed to be king. Now as you know, you became king by marrying the right woman. The heiress. The woman who had the pure royal blood flowing through her veins. It was matriarchal—matrilineal. And sometimes a queen could even rule, and it becomes matriarchal. And you'll see that happens at the end of this dynasty. So we get Amenmesses, who was not the king's eldest son—who was usually the one who marries this right woman. He's a son of Merneptah, but he's not supposed to be king. And all of a sudden—boom! He's king. He has a tomb in the Valley of the Kings. So there's no doubt he was ruling as king. But we don't know much about him. He's succeeded by Seti II, probably his brother.

Now what does Seti II do? The first thing he does is erase Amenmesses's name wherever he finds it. Now why would a king do that? Well there are some reasons. One theory and it's just a theory is that Seti II is the king. He was supposed to be king—he's the prince who was supposed to be king. And it may be Amenmesses somehow pushed him aside, or something like that. But it's clear he doesn't like him. So he erases his name. Now this was common in Egypt by the way. Pharaohs erasing the names of predecessors. Common. It's an interesting practice. They did it for two reasons. One was, when you really wanted to erase all traces of anyone. The Egyptians didn't have a concept of heaven and hell. They just had heaven, the next world. The worst thing that could happen to you is if you went out of existence. There was no place where you went for eternal torment. No. You went out of existence. That was the worst. For example, in the "Book of the Dead" when you're being judged to see if you're worthy, if you're not worthy of going to the next world, they just take your heart out and throw it to this creature who's a devourer of hearts, and you go out of existence. So one reason was if you hated your predecessor for some reason, you would erase his name wherever it existed. And to erase the name, you erased him. He no longer existed. And that's what happened, remember, at the end of Tutankhamen's reign when you had the heretic pharaoh—his father, Akhenaten. And everybody associated with that was annihilated from the records. So I think that's probably why Seti does this.

The other reason why you might erase another pharaoh's name and replace it with yours, is you wanted to take credit for his monument. Ramses the Great was called "The Great Chiseler." Why? Because he erased everybody else's name. Not because he hated them, he wanted to take credit for all the monuments. So for example, we get statues that were 100 years old during Ramses's time, with his name on them. He would take a statue, carve out the previous pharaoh's name, and put his. And the idea was kind of like when the gods looked down, they would see this statue, and they would see it has Ramses's name, and they would credit Ramses. You know, they could look down and look at the statue. But they wouldn't look down and see that Ramses was carving out somebody else's name. It's an interesting concept. But that's why people did this all the time in Egypt. It makes it very difficult for Egyptologists. Just because you find a statue with somebody's name on it, doesn't mean it's of him. Very often we know it's not.

So Seti comes in, eradicates his brother's name. Now Seti had three queens—two of them are going to be important for us. We're coming to the end of the dynasty. We're coming to the end. There's only going to be two more rulers. But he has three queens, of whom two are important. Now remember, please, that there were three relationships a woman could have with regard to the pharaoh. "Great Wife." That was only one at any one time. She was the honcho of the harim. Then there were queens who were kind of married; they were a wife, married to the pharaoh—or you could be a concubine. So three relationships. So he has three queens. Three wives, so to speak. Now one is Tia. She is going to be the mother of the next king. And another one, Towsret, is going to actually rule Egypt. So Seti's got some interesting women around him. Interesting.

But he builds his own monuments. Seti built a chapel at Karnak, and let me tell you about this chapel. Karnak Temple was the largest religious building in the history of the world. Huge. For thousands of years each pharaoh went to this place and added his own temple. Don't think of it as one temple. It doesn't make any sense, the plan. You can get lost in Karnak Temple. Because it's Ramses's buildings, Seti's buildings, Seti II's buildings. Everybody added. This was sacred ground. This was the Vatican of Egypt. And Seti II goes to Karnak Temple and he builds a special monument. A boat chapel.

Now let me explain what a boat chapel was. Remember in Thebes, that the chief gods were Amun, Mut, and Khonsu. Egyptian gods always came in trinities. Amun is "the Hidden One," Mut is his wife, and Khonsu is their child. Well at Karnak Temple statues of these gods were kept. And these statues were never seen by the commoners. No. They're kept in the back of the temple in the holy of holies. But at festival times the statues were placed on portable shrines in the shape of a boat. These are pretty big boats. I mean like about 20 feet long. And the boat shrine rested on poles—two poles. And during festivals, the priests—shaven headed priests, 10 on each side sometimes—would carry these poles on their shoulders. And they would parade the statues of the gods in front of the people. And for the first time in a long time, people could see the statues of their gods. It was a big deal. Now Seti II builds a boat chapel. It's a small temple. By small—it's probably 40 feet across maybe. But it has three compartments. One for the boat of Amun. One for the boat of Mut. One for the boat of Khonsu. So during festivals, the statues would be placed in the shrine, the boats would be taken out of the shrine, and paraded for the people to see. So that is his monument that we know he built at Karnak Temple.

Then he dies. And he is succeeded by his son Siptah, who is the son of one of his wives, Tia. Siptah is an interesting mummy. We have his mummy. He's another one of those that was found in that royal cache. The foot is deformed, probably from polio. Many people think that Siptah had polio. And the foot is deformed. And I think it's interesting that a pharaoh of Egypt could have a deformity. I mean he became king of Egypt, no question about it. Siptah is king of Egypt with a deformed foot. Could he lead the army? Well, from a chariot, perhaps. But it also may be a sign that Egypt is weakening. That they're going to accept a pharaoh with a defect, with a birth defect. Or a defect of any kind. But Siptah becomes king of Egypt. Doesn't reign long. Maybe five years. Something like that.

And then it happens. The thing I mentioned. His stepmother, Towsret, becomes ruler of Egypt. We don't know why. She is on the throne. We do not know why. Only two years. She even had a small tomb in the Valley of the Kings. So she was definitely ruling. There was a separate little tomb for her jewelry. Quite interesting. They found silver gloves in it. Silver gloves—I don't mean the color. Silver gloves. And eight finger rings. Beautiful finger rings. So she had her jewelry hidden in a cache for eternity. But the XIXth Dynasty ends in this very strange way, with a woman ruling Egypt. Next time we'll see the consequences of what happens when a woman rules Egypt. I'll see you then.

Lecture Thirty-Four
Dynasty XX—The Decline Continues

Scope:

After a brief attempt to restore Egypt's stability during the reign of Ramses III, the downward slide continues. We will discuss who the mysterious Sea Peoples were and how they contributed to the weakening of Egypt. We will closely examine the reign of Ramses III to see glimpses of the subsequent decline.

Outline

I. Setnakht, "Set is victorious" (1185–1182 B.C.), is a mystery. Who was he?

   A. As soon as he became king, Setnakht erased Twosret's name from her tomb in the Valley of the Kings.

   B. Papyrus Harris, 113 feet long and dated the day Ramses III died, gives some other clues about him.

      1. The papyrus was supposed to be buried with Ramses III but was found in a private tomb in 1855. Perhaps the robbers of Ramses III's tomb found the papyrus and sold it as a Book of the Dead. Because most of them couldn't read, they may not have even known it was a historical papyrus.

      2. The papyrus tells of the beginning of the dynasty. Setnakht put down Asiatic rebellions, reopened temples, and restored order.

II. Ramses III (1182–1151 B.C.) was perhaps the last great Egyptian pharaoh.

   A. The Libyans tried to invade (year 5), but Ramses crushed them.

   B. The Sea Peoples, a confederation of Philistines, Sicilians, and other Mediterranean peoples, also attempted to invade Egypt.

      1. For them, this was a period of large-scale emigration. On walls are carved depictions of women and children in ox carts.

      2. A land battle repelled them at the border of Egypt.

3. At the mouth of the Nile, a landlocked sea battle favored the Egyptians, who were not great sailors. Again, the Sea Peoples were repelled.

C. Papyrus Harris tells of Ramses's great achievements.
  1. He gave immense gifts to the temples: land, cattle, cloth, oil, wine.
  2. Numerous successful military campaigns were chronicled.
  3. The economy of Egypt was described as booming.

D. Medinet Habu, Ramses's mortuary temple, served different purposes.
  1. Its main function was as a mortuary temple where Ramses could be worshipped after his death.
  2. It has fortress-like towers that show a Syrian influence.
  3. Medinet Habu was also used as a palace when Ramses was in Thebes for official occasions.

E. Ramses III buried his sons Amunhirkepshef and Khaemwaset in the Valley of the Queens. (These are also the names of the sons of Ramses the Great [II]; Ramses III was unrelated to Ramses the Great but wanted to be like him.)

F. The Harem Conspiracy Papyrus tells of a plot by one of Ramses's queens to kill her husband so her son could become king.
  1. Magic was used to try to kill Ramses.
  2. More than two dozen conspirators close to the king were convicted.
  3. The records indicate that Ramses died before the conspirators were executed.

G. Ramses's tomb (KV 11) was intended for Setnakht originally but abandoned when it hit another tomb. Good spaces in the Valley were running out.
  1. There is an unusual secular scene of two harpists painted on the tomb wall. Because James Bruce discovered it in 1769, it has been called "Bruce's tomb."
  2. Ramses's mummy, found in the Deir el Bahri cache, became the model for mummy movies.
  3. Ramses III was succeeded by three sons.

III. Ramses IV, the first son to succeed, ruled for just six years (1151–1145 B.C.).

A. He was the son of Ramses III, so his claim to the throne was legitimate.

B. He sent workers to the Wadi Hammamat for black granite to make statues of the gods, a sign of prosperity.

IV. Ramses V (1145–1141 B.C.) was another legitimate successor with a short reign.

A. He was another son of Ramses III.

B. His mummy has spots on the face that suggest smallpox.

V. Ramses VI (1141–1133 B.C.) was probably a weak ruler.

A. He was the third son of Ramses III to become king.

B. Foreign territories were slipping away during his reign; the turquoise mines were abandoned.

VI. Ramses VII (1133–1126 B.C.) was a grandson of Ramses III.

A. The son of Ramses VI, he saw the decline of the dynasty continue.

B. There was economic turmoil in Egypt, and prices soared.

VII. Not a great deal is known of the next several pharaohs.

A. Ramses VIII (1126 B.C.) ruled for only a year, and little is known of him.

B. Ramses IX ruled from 1126–1108 B.C.
   1. He had a long reign, during which the royal tombs were robbed.
   2. The king could no longer protect the Valley. Depositions by participants even date the tomb robbing.

C. Of Ramses X (1108–1098 B.C.) little is known, other than that all foreign territories were lost during his reign.

VIII. Ramses XI (1098–1070 B.C.) was the last of the dynasty.

A. The "Tale of Wenamum" aptly describes the times. Wenamum, an official, was sent to Byblos to buy cedarwood but was robbed and treated poorly, a sign of the declining reputation of the kingdom. He procured the wood but only after waiting for months.

B. The "Tale of Wenamum" refers to Heri-Hor, the powerful high priest of Amun who took control of Egypt.
   1. He first held the office of viceroy to Kush.

2. He decorated the Temple of Khonsu at Karnak and is shown to be the same size as the king.
3. In year 24, he wrote his name in a cartouche.

C. He ruled in the south while Ramses XI ruled from the Delta.

D. He called the years of his reign "repetition of births," literally *renaissance*.

Essential Reading:

N. K. Sandars, *The Sea Peoples*.

Supplementary Reading:

Peter A. Clayton, *Chronicle of the Pharaohs*, pp. 160–171.

Questions to Consider:

1. What new indications of a decline do we get in this dynasty?
2. What must have been the main concern of Ramses III?

Lecture Thirty Four—Transcript
Dynasty XX—The Decline Continues

Hi. Welcome back. Remember last time we talked about the XIXth Dynasty. And we saw it declining from the great years of Ramses down to a woman, Twosret, ruling Egypt. The decline continues in the next dynasty. And I want to talk about that dynasty—Dynasty XX. There are going to be some interesting things here. We're going to see mysterious peoples trying to invade Egypt; the "Sea Peoples." And we'll see Egypt weakening. And we'll also look at the reign of one pharaoh carefully, Ramses III, to see what indications there are of this decline.

But let's start with the first pharaoh, Setnakht. His name? It means something, as you've gathered by now. *Seth* is the god Seth; *nakht* means "mighty" or "victorious." So his name is something like "Seth is victorious" or "Seth is mighty." He's a mystery king; I can hardly tell you anything about him. The one thing I can tell you, is that as soon as he becomes king, he erases Twosret's name from her tomb in the Valley of the Kings. She is the queen who rules and then is erased as quickly as it happened—a sign that there was turmoil. Now, Setnakht has this tomb in the Valley of the Kings, we know that. There's only one other source that we really find out about him from. It's the Papyrus Harris. And it's a curious story about this papyrus.

Now papyri, as you know, are named after the people who discover them or own them. So Harris owns this papyrus. It's a papyrus that is written during the reign of the next pharaoh, Ramses III—Ramses Mery-Amun. He's going to be the next pharaoh. And it was supposed to be buried with Ramses III. It's a history of his reign. But it turned up in a private person's tomb—in a commoner's tomb. Now how does a royal papyrus—the archive of Ramses III—turn up in the tomb of a commoner? I'll give you my theory. Just a theory, but I think it's a good bet.

Ramses III is buried in his tomb in the Valley of the Kings. And we'll get to that. Buried in the tomb, with his papyrus. The archive of his reign. That tomb is robbed some time later. The papyrus is stolen. Now the papyrus has no intrinsic value. It's paper basically. But the robber figures out a way to sell it. Now remember, that most people in Egypt are illiterate. Very few can read. Only scribes. And the robber probably doesn't know what this thing says even. So he figures out, I'll sell it as a "Book of the Dead." Now many wealthy Egyptians were buried with "Books of the Dead." These are papyri intended to help your journey to the next world, to assure that you'll make it successfully. So it's sold as this record. This administrative record is sold to somebody. And here's a "Book of the Dead." You can be buried with this thing. And somebody went to the next world thinking he had a "Book of the Dead." But he really had administrative records of Ramses III. But this papyrus is a clue to Setnakht's reign.

Ramses III records his reign. But he says the previous pharaoh, Setnakht, probably dad whom he's glorifying, repulsed the Asiatics who had tried to enter Egypt. He says he restored the order. So at least Ramses III is saying, Setnakht did pretty good stuff. He took over when things were rough—remember, a queen ended the previous dynasty, ruling, took over, and got things on track. So at least in this papyrus it says, Setnakht was pretty good. Otherwise I can't tell you much about this mystery king. But now we get Ramses III. And for him, we've got lots of stories. Now I think in some sense Ramses III is the last great pharaoh of Egypt. He does great things, and let's talk about those things.

First the Libyans tried to invade Egypt. Ramses III repulses them— crushes them. That's about the fifth year of his reign. So he's not ruling very long and he's got this battle, but he does it. And then he talks about the "Sea Peoples." Now they're just called the "Sea Peoples." They seem to be a confederation of Mediterranean people, Mediterranean types. They're probably Philistines. Even people, perhaps, from the area of Sicily. And it looks like they were having hard times in their own lands. Because they're emigrating. They're trying to come into Egypt. And we have scenes of them carved on walls. And they have ox carts, large carts drawn by oxen, and they're piled high with their possessions. And you see women and children coming along. So this is not just a military invasion. This is a real immigration. It's like, maybe, the United States at the beginning of the century—hard times. People want to come in.

Ramses III views it certainly as an invasion. There were military people with them. And there are two major battles that he fights against these Sea Peoples. The first is on land, towards the Delta. Remember the Delta is that moist area of Egypt. Look at it as a hand. Imagine it as a hand. The Nile flows from south to north. And then at the end of it, you have a hand with different branches of the Nile, where the Nile spreads out and flows into the Mediterranean. So on one of those branches he keeps out the Sea Peoples. So he fights them on land. Well and good. But then there's a battle on "sea." Now "sea" is really—I say it in quotes. It's in the Delta. On one of the branches of the Nile. So it's really almost a landlocked battle. And that's fortunate for the Egyptians. Very fortunate. Remember, they were not good sailors. They were spoiled by the Nile. It was so easy to sail the Nile that they really never learned difficult maneuvers. For example, if you were sailing from south to north the way the current goes, you just went with the current. You had some oars, for steering, but you didn't have to have to propel your boat. If you were going from north to south against the current? Well there's a prevailing wind at your back. You put up your sails. And you go. So they never had to do the really difficult stuff like tacking or learning navigation. So they weren't good sailors.

So when it comes to the battle at sea, they were lucky. They didn't have to maneuver. It's on this little area. Basically, they were fighting a land battle from ships. And the scenes of it that Ramses carved shows that. You have archers. They're on the deck of a ship, shooting arrows at the other guys, the bad guys, who were pretty close to them. You even see guys jumping ship from one to another. So this is a land battle fought on ships. And of course, as you know, the Egyptians are always victorious. So the Sea Peoples are repelled.

Now this Papyrus Harris that I told you about, it tells about Ramses's achievements. And there were many. He really was a great pharaoh. First of all, it lists all the gifts that he gave to the temples of Egypt. Now, this is important. One of the things the pharaoh did—it was a kind of business agreement between the king and the gods—was when you went out and battled and you were successful, you brought back booty. And you donated a lot of it to the temples, because the gods had looked upon you favorably with your battle. So Ramses lists all of the gifts he gives to the temple, and it's an immense quantity of—oils; priests needed oils. Linen—priests wore white linen only. Linens. Land. Land is crucial. By the end of this dynasty, the temple of Amun at Thebes is going to own 90 percent of all the temple lands in Egypt. It's a vast tract of land. And they didn't own just the land. They had the cattle. The produce. Everything. And Papyrus Harris lists all of this. So we can see that Ramses is living during an economic boom. Powerful. Giving to the temples and getting back. He's conquering foreign lands. So Papyrus Harris is an important source. Also he lists his military campaigns—all of them successful, of course. And we know from this papyrus that Egypt is really booming. It gives you an accurate picture. He's really doing fine. Now what happens during his reign is really curious. There are certain signs of decline. But first, let's look at the high point.

His temple. He builds a temple called Medinet Habu. Now that's the modern Arabic name for it. It's really called "United With Eternity." This is a mortuary temple. Ramses is going to be united with eternity. Now remember what a mortuary temple is. It's a place where the pharaoh is going to be worshipped after his death. We are going to have priests forever—forever!—bringing food, beer, bread, to the temple for the soul of Ramses. And the way Ramses assures it, is he gives land to the temple. And forever the produce of that land will sort of be an endowment to his mortuary temple.

Now the mortuary temple is unique. Unique. It's huge, first of all. I mean it is huge. The walls are 30 feet thick. Built out of stone, not mud brick. Temples had to last forever. Palaces, houses, just a generation—they were built out of mud brick. Temples, tombs, out of stone. It's huge. But it had three functions. Not just the mortuary temple. If you look at the entranceway to Medinet Habu, you will see that it's in the shape of a Syrian fortress. It's very much like a Syrian fortress. Ramses obviously thought that at some point he was going to have to defend Egypt in the south, maybe, where the temple is in Thebes on the Western Bank. Remember he's kicked out Libyans, he's kicked out the Sea Peoples, he's seen it all happen. So he builds his mortuary temple to have a double function as a fortress. There are places on the top where archers could stand behind crenellations—those little bumps, you know—and shoot their arrows. So first, it's the only mortuary temple we have that looks like a fort.

Another function—it had a palace. Ramses actually lived there, but not permanently. He's ruling from the north; the capital is in the north. He lived there when there were religious festivals. He would come south for the festival of Opet. Now that was the greatest festival in Egypt at the time. It's when the statues of the gods, Amun, Mut and Khonsu—the trinity of Thebes—were taken out and brought from Karnak Temple about a mile and a half away, to Luxor Temple. And they would stay there for a fortnight. And during that time, there would be feasting, and all kinds of partying. And he would come for that festival. And where would he stay? He's not going to stay at a hotel. He had his own palace built.

And it's interesting to walk the palace. One of the things that amazes people when they see the palace of Ramses III, a great king of Egypt, is how small it is. There are no great rooms. And the reason is, there's nothing architecturally that enables you to build a room in those days. You can't have a large piece of stone spanning a roof. There was no way to support a large open area. So it's really a cramped area. And when you look at Ramses's bathroom, it's practically camping out. I mean, it's like a latrine. That's the room that Ramses III is going to use. It's a typical king's bathroom. But it's not very impressive. But this is a palace, it's a fortress, and it's the mortuary temple of Ramses.

Now Ramses, during his lifetime, saw some of his sons die also. Just like Ramses the Great, remember. But one of the things we have to keep clear. Ramses III is the XXth Dynasty. Ramses the Great is the XIXth Dynasty. They are not related in any way whatsoever. Ramses III has chosen his name because he wants to hearken back to the days when Ramses the Great was ruling. So he kind of wants association by name. And he does it doubly. He buried some of his children, too. He reigned for about 30 years. And he buried some of his children. And two of the children whom he buries in the Valley of the Queens—now remember, the Valley of the Queens is a little bit of a misnomer. It's what the guides call it today. But it wasn't just queens, it was princes also. And two of his children that he buries there are Amunhirkepshef and Khaemwaset. Now, those names should sound familiar. Those are the names of two of the children of Ramses the Great. Remember? Amunhirkepshef was the firstborn son who may have died during the Exodus. Khaemwaset was the over-achieving archaeologist. High Priest of Memphis. So Ramses III is naming his kids after the kids of Ramses the Great. He wants this association. And to some extent it works. He is a great king. He is. So he buries his kids there. But during his reign, we have something that's really unique in Egyptian history. There is a plot to kill him.

It's called the "Harim Conspiracy." One of his queens plotted to kill him by magic. Now how do we know about such a thing? Ramses isn't going to put this on his temple wall. We have a papyrus that is in a sense a stenographer's transcript. It is a court record of what happened. The conspirators, nearly two dozen of them, were tried. And we have some of the details of the conspiracy—how do you kill a pharaoh by black magic?

Well first, it involved a queen, as I say. And she was plotting to kill Ramses because she wanted her son to become pharaoh. And this is not that unusual, that queens wanted their kids to become the next pharaoh. And maybe, if the pharaoh is dead, now mine can move in quickly. So she's plotting. And it involved priests of the temple. Now why priests? They had the Books of Magic. They were the ones who knew how to do this by magic. So we have priests involved, we have palace guards involved, we have the queen involved. It's called the "Harim Conspiracy."

Now we know that they were convicted. What is the penalty? Well, in Egypt there were various penalties. Jail—incarceration—is a fairly modern concept. The ancient world didn't throw people in jail for doing bad things. It didn't make sense. Somebody does something bad, so you put them somewhere and you support them? Why do that? It's sort of a strain on your resources. Rather, punish them in a way that it's over with. Boom. Finished. Now for example, in Egypt if it was a not too too heinous crime, you could cut off ears, or a nose. And that way, not only would you have punished them, but everybody would know, watch out for this guy, he's a crook. If it was a really serious crime, you would execute them. And the Egyptians executed by impaling someone on a stake. Not a nice way to go. So these conspirators had a variety. Some had probably ears cut off, noses cut off. But some were certainly executed, as far as we can tell from the record. Now, the record is damaged.

Ramses III died before the trial was over. Now I'm not suggesting from black magic, that he dies from the magic. But he dies before the trial was over. And the people are probably executed after he dies. He is buried in the Valley of the Kings. Now, his tomb is rather unusual. Pharaohs always had religious scenes on the walls of their tombs. They never had these daily life scenes. You know when you look in the Egyptian art books, and you see people in the fields plowing, you see people fishing and hunting. Those are not the tombs of the kings. No. Those are the tombs of the nobles. They wanted to show the gods what they liked in this world, so it would be continued in the next. Kings had to put religious texts on their walls.

Now there's one unusual thing about Ramses III's tomb. One. There's a secular scene. He apparently was a music lover. And in a side chapel, it shows two men playing the harp. They're playing the harp. And they're blind. Very often in Egypt, harpers were shown as blind. The idea was, that blind people are perhaps more sensitive to sound, so they went into music. So we have this scene of two harpers who were blind. And this is a tomb that was seen by a guy named James Bruce who was looking for the source of the Nile in the early part of the 19th century. He came into this tomb, he saw the harpers, and he told the world about it. And it became known as "Bruce's Tomb." To this day, some people say, oh, it's "Bruce's Tomb." Other people who don't know it's Ramses III call it the "Tomb of the Two Harpers."

So Ramses III is buried in his tomb. His mummy, by the way—a little bit of Egyptological trivia—his mummy was found in the Deir el Bahri cache. And if you look closely at the mummy, it'll look familiar to you. Why? Many of the mummy movies, they patterned the mummy after Ramses III. And I'll tell you a little detail you could look for. Not the Boris Karloff movie. The famous 1932 Boris Karloff movie That's not Ramses III. But after that movie, there were quite a few sequels, because Universal Studios did so well with it that they brought out three more movies—*The Mummy's Tomb, The Mummy's Curse, The Mummy's Hand*. And they were patterning the mummy after Ramses III. Now Ramses III's mummy had been damaged by tomb robbers. And when it was refurbished in ancient times, the head had come off the body. So they put a stick kind of where the neck is, put it back on. But they wrapped a big bandage around it to cover that the neck was damaged. So if you look at the mummy movies, the mummy always has this big—kind of looks like a scarf almost—around its neck. That's because Ramses III's mummy was damaged. But that's Ramses III's mummy. A little bit of Egyptological trivia for you.

Now, Ramses III leaves us with a little bit of a mystery. Rules for about 30 years. But if you'll look at his temple, Medinet Habu, "United With Eternity," where all his great deeds are written on the wall and there's a wonderful long, long list of the dedications of things he gave to the temple. Fantastic. I mean it goes for 150 feet. Just list after list of oils and gold and this and that. But if you look carefully, and read what's on the temple walls, it only tells about the first 11 years of his reign. There is nothing about the last two decades that he ruled for. That may be a sign that things were starting to go downhill. Think about it. There was a plot to kill him. He couldn't have been that secure on his throne. So it looks like even during the time of Ramses III, things are slipping away. I mean it could be that Egypt is going downhill already. He is succeeded by three sons of his, all named Ramses. Now everybody in this dynasty from now on is going to be named Ramses. But remember, there's no relation to Ramses the Great. They're just calling themselves Ramses.

The three sons? You've got Ramses IV. Now he rules for about six years. And the good thing—the sign that there's still a little bit of wealth left, a little bit of power—he sends an expedition to the Wadi Hammamat. Now the Wadi Hammamat is a long march from Thebes towards the Red Sea across a desert. It requires organization. You've got to dig wells. Why does he send an expedition there? Black granite is there. He wants the black stones for sarcophagi, for buildings, for temples. And it's hard. But he sends an expedition. So at least there's a sign there's still stability. Things may be slipping away, but there's some stability. And if you go to the Wadi Hammamat—and tourists hardly ever go there, because there's no reason, except to go to where the black granite is. Fantastic inscriptions on the rocks. Fantastic. These expeditions were sometimes a couple of thousand men. And they knew how to quarry stone. These guys were stone workers. So very often, they wanted to pray. They were religious people. But they didn't have a temple there. So right on the rock, they would carve a statue of their god. And some of them are beautiful. And they would list all the men of the expedition. Under the vizier so-and-so we came. We quarried so much stone. And they could go there and pray every day, when they were finished with their work. So it's rather beautiful. It's in the middle of the desert. And you're just driving along this desert road. It used to be the old caravan route, nobody takes it anymore. And then all of a sudden you come in this valley. You've got black stones on either side, and they're all inscribed with beautiful hieroglyphs. It's really spectacular.

So at least a son of Ramses III is able to send an expedition to the Wadi Hammamat. The other son, Ramses V, he's a legitimate successor, but we don't know much about him. I'll tell you the one interesting thing about his mummy though, he has spots on his face. We're pretty sure he had smallpox. The earliest case of smallpox recorded. And Ramses VI, the other son of Ramses III, doesn't reign too long. But we do know one thing. Egypt is starting to slip out from under him. Foreign territories are lost. They no longer send mining expeditions to the Sinai for turquoise. They don't have the power. The army isn't there. Something is happening. During the next reign, Ramses VII, there's an economic turmoil. Prices soar. Inflation. They had inflation, just like we do. And it soared. Ramses VIII, we hardly know anything about. Hardly anything. Now Ramses IX, he has a pretty long reign. But the only thing we know really for his reign—there were tomb robbers. This is when the royal tombs are robbed. This is when we start to get real robbing in the Valley of the Kings.

And think of what that means. They could no longer protect the Valley. I mean, this is where you have the body of Ramses the Great and the body of Ramses III. The bodies of these great kings. And they're being plundered. And how do I know that it's during Ramses IX's reign? We have some court records. I'll give you an idea of what they said. They took sort of what we would call depositions. There are records. This is during the reign of Ramses IX. They got the thieves, they caught them. And this is what one of them is saying: "We found the burial place of the royal wife, his royal wife. We forced it open. We opened their outer coffins, and their inner coffins in which they lay. We found this noble mummy of this king, equipped like a warrior. A large number of sacred eye amulets and ornaments of gold were at his neck. And his head piece of gold was on him." So the thieves found this royal tomb intact. "The noble mummy of this king was all covered with gold. And his inner coffins were bedizened with gold and silver, inside and outside, with inlays of all kinds of precious stones. We appropriated the gold which we found on the noble mummy of this god. And his eye amulets his ornaments which were around his neck. And in the coffins in which he lay, we found the royal wife likewise. And we took all that we found on her too. We set fire to their inner coffins. We stole their outfit, which we found on them consisting of objects of gold silver bronze and divided them up among ourselves. We made this gold which we found on these two gods into eight parts." So there were probably eight robbers. Now this is a concerted effort all together. And they took the gold. But they were caught. But this happens during the reign of Ramses IX. So we know that Egypt is really going downhill rather quickly. I mean it's a sad story to see Egypt go down from the time of greatness, to where the mummies are just being robbed.

Ramses X is the next king. Another mummy, another pharaoh. Unimportant. All we know is, that all foreign territories are lost during his reign. But now we come to the last king of the dynasty— Ramses XI. And we get a few strange things during his reign. First, we have a papyrus from his time, which was originally thought to be more literary than historic, but it's probably historical. It's called the "Tale of Wenamun." Now Wenamun was an official. And he was sent to Byblos to bring back wood—cedar. Now why is he going to bring back cedars of Lebanon? Well first of all, you need it for the pharaoh's ships. That's important. Because there are no forests in Egypt. You're not going to get timber out of Egypt. But also, remember I told you last time about those royal barks that the shrines—where the statues were put on and carried—that looked like boats? You need it for that. And you need doors for the temples; big doors. So Wenamun is sent. This is during the reign of the last king of this dynasty.

And what happens to Wenamun? First of all, he's robbed along the way. The king's ambassador is robbed. It never would have happened during the time of greatness—never. So then he arrives at Byblos. And what does he say to the prince of Byblos that he has to go before. He says, "Well, give me the cedars of Lebanon anyway. I have a statue of Amun." By the way he took a statue of Amun with him, who was called "Amun of the Road." It's the equivalent of our St. Christopher. The patriot saint of travelers. He has this little statue called "Amun of the Road." And he says to the prince, "I've brought you Amun." And the prince says, "Thanks a lot, but where's the money?" And Wenamun is trying to be eloquent, he says, "You know, our pharaohs have done business with you for many many generations." And he says, "Yeah. You're right. You're right. You're right. But they always paid. Where is the money?" Wenamun is in a tight spot. He really is. Eventually, somehow he talks the prince of Byblos into giving him the wood, the cedars, probably the king sends money. Eventually. But he waited for almost a year. He's waiting there. For months and months and months. And finally the cedars are felled. They wait by the river until they're loaded on ships, and finally he returns.

But one of the things that is curious about this document. We're certain that he's sent during the reign of Ramses XI. But he doesn't talk about Ramses XI. He talks about another guy, Heri-Hor. And this is something that happens during the reign of Ramses XI that is shocking. Never in the time of a pharaoh had this happened. A high priest of Amun, by the name of Heri-Hor, builds his own temple at Karnak Temple. Dedicated to Khonsu, the son of Amun and Mut. And shows himself on the temple as large as the king—as large as the king. Not only that, a little later on in the reign, year 24 of Ramses XI, he writes his name in a cartouche. This high priest of Amun writes his name in a cartouche which symbolizes the king's power. We have the high priest of Amun claiming that he is the king of Egypt. Now, how is this possible? Well remember, Ramses XI is ruling in the north. Out of the capital in the north. Things are slipping away. He may have all he can handle in the north. So Heri-Hor, this high priest, calls himself king.

And we end this dynasty with two people writing their names in cartouches. Ramses XI and Heri-Hor. But Heri-Hor adds one little thing to his name—"repetition of births." And what he is saying is, that there is going to be a "renaissance" under me. Things are going to get better. And we'll talk about that next time. See you then.

Lecture Thirty-Five
Ancient Egyptian Magic

Scope:

In the last lecture, we saw a plot to kill a pharaoh by magic—an indication of just how central magic was to the ancient Egyptian. We will try to distinguish magic from religion—not an easy task—and will then examine the three basic elements of magic: (1) the spell, (2) the ritual, and (3) the magician. After we have a clear definition of magic, we will look at different magical practices.

Outline

I. We have already discussed the differences between mythology, philosophy, and religion (Lecture Three). Now we consider magic. Magic and religion, although they have many similarities, are very different.

   A. The supernatural element is present in both magic and religion: each tries to deal with events beyond the laws of physics. We might call this *parapsychology* today. In religion, we call such events *miracles*.

   B. Magic is always goal-oriented; prayer or devotion, on the other hand, doesn't have to have a specific objective, because belief itself is sufficient. The difference between a magician and a priest is that the magician is the agent of change, while the priest is an intermediary.

   C. The Egyptians had plenty of both religion and magic. They had, for example, a goddess of magic, Heka. (Most of the gods associated with magic were women.) Isis, too, had magic capability, as in "She Who Knows Everyone's Name." Egyptians often had two names—one of them, public; the other known only by one's mother.

II. There are three basic elements of magic.

   A. The spell, the spoken part of magic, has its own logic. The spell obeyed certain principles. A critical precept was: *the word is the deed.*

B. The ritual involves a physical performance, such as burning incense or drawing a protective circle—in this way it resembles theater.

    1. Some spells, for example, prevented one from being bitten by a scorpion at night.

    2. To enforce such spells, the Egyptians had magical wands made of bone or ivory to make a magic circle and complete the ritual.

C. Magicians were heroic, because they controlled the forces of nature. There were priest magicians associated with traditional temples (in the Old Testament, pharaoh called for his priest magicians, or "scribes of the house of life") and lay magicians, especially in rural areas.

III. Magical practices varied considerably, depending on the desired goal.

  A. Egyptians were resurrectionists and viewed the next world as much like this one, only better. They believed that labor would still be needed in the next world.

    1. Servant statues, called *ushabtis ("I'm answering")*, were intended to come to life in the next world and do work for the deceased.

    2. Some Egyptians buried 365 such statues, standing with arms crossed and inscribed with magical spells. Some *ushabtis* were made from the quartzite paste *faience*.

    3. Many *ushabtis* have magical spells from the Book of the Dead. (The sorcerer's apprentice scene from Disney's *Fantasia* recalls this.)

    4. For every 10 *ushabtis*, there was an overseer who was not required to do manual labor.

  B. Oracle statues could tell the future and were said to be capable of talking and deciding legal cases. One record tells of an oracle statue "solving" a crime.

  C. The most dominant form of magic in ancient Egypt was amulets, small ornaments worn for protection. The Egyptians had different amulets for the living and for the dead.

    1. The Eye of Horus amulet was worn for good health. Our pharmacists' Rx is a corruption of the Eye.

    2. The scarab (beetle) was probably the most common amulet. It represented continued existence. (The

Egyptians believed the scarab could procreate without both sexes being present.)

3. Surprisingly, the ankh (a looped cross), which stood for life, was the rarest of all amulets.
4. The Djed Pillar amulet represented the backbone of Osiris and was primarily for the dead.
5. Not only shape but also color and material were considerations in making amulets.

Essential Reading:

Bob Brier, *Ancient Egyptian Magic*.

Supplementary Reading:

Wallis Budge, *Egyptian Magic*.

Questions to Consider:

1. What are the three basic elements of magic?
2. How does magic differ from religion?

Lecture Thirty Five—Transcript
Ancient Egyptian Magic

Hello. I'm glad you're back. Last time we talked about the end of the XXth Dynasty. And we saw Ramses III as the last great pharaoh of that dynasty. But even in his reign, if you'll remember, they tried to kill him by magic. Magic was so central to the ancient Egyptian world that I want to take a little bit of a chronological detour today. I want to not continue chronologically for the pharaohs, but I want to talk just about magic, and what magic was to the Egyptians.

Now I'll try to do a couple of things—one is very hard. And that's— I want to try to distinguish between magic and religion. Not easy. And the other thing I will do is, I will show you the different aspects of magic, how it had to have a spell, how there was a ritual, and how there was a magician. And you sort of needed all three to make it work.

But let me ask you to go back to almost our first lecture. Remember where I tried to make the distinction between the kinds of thoughts that the Egyptians had? And that there was mythology, which was stories that you're supposed to listen to. Not take literally, but there's some deep message. Mythology tries to answer questions like, how does the world begin? Is there life after death? And then there was religion, which also tries to answer those very same questions. Life after death. Creation. But it did in a different way. It didn't have tales that you're not supposed to believe. It tells you stories that take place in historical time—like the Exodus. So religion and mythology are quite different. One is not to be believed literally, the other you're supposed to really believe it. And then there was philosophy—I didn't mention philosophy—is the third. And try to make a distinction there. Philosophy tries to answer the same questions. Is there life after death? How did the world begin? But it does it in a different way—with logic. It requires proof. In religion, you just need belief. You can say, I believe in that, and that ends it. But in philosophy, we have to supply more of a story.

So I tried to make those distinctions to see what did the Egyptians do? Did they do philosophy? Did they do religion? Did they do mythology? I think the answer up to this point is they certainly had plenty of mythology; that we know. They certainly had religion. Plenty of gods. But philosophy—we haven't seen any real papyri that are really philosophical in the sense that we mean it today. So maybe they really didn't do philosophy. But that's a story for another day.

Now I want to try to do something similar. Delineate magic from religion. Now, let's start with what they have in common. I think magic and religion both involve the supernatural. Now what do I mean by the supernatural? What I mean is, they each try to deal with things that are beyond the laws of physics. Now today in modern terms, what would you class all this as in modern scientific jargon? Parapsychology. Parapsychology is the science that studies things like ESP, precognition, things like that. Well all of those things—and if you look at the definition of parapsychology, it's—parapsychology studies those things that are beyond the laws of physics. So in other words, if the laws of physics can't explain it, then parapsychology studies it.

I think it's the same with religion. And magic. Both religion and magic involve phenomena that go beyond the laws of physics. Like for example, the parting of the Sea of Reeds in the Exodus. I think in religion the word really most used for those phenomena that go beyond the laws of physics—miracles. That's what a miracle is. It's something beyond the laws of physics. The same with magic. If you've got a magician pulling a rabbit out of a hat, it's beyond the laws of physics. But there's got to be a difference between the two of them. I mean we do sense there's a difference. I think everybody feels that religion is different from magic. And I want to try—and I say it's very hard—to make that distinction.

First, let me give you one difference at least that I think is different. In magic, you always have a goal. You always do magic. Say a spell; perform a ritual with a particular end in sight. You want to bring something about. But in prayer—I think it's possible just to pray for the sake of praying. You don't have to pray for something. You simply can pray. So I think one difference is magic is always goal-oriented. Religion isn't. You can simply believe.

Now I think there's anther distinction, and this is the hard one, very hard to make. I think the difference between a magician and a priest is that the magician, when he brings about the result—you know he's got his cape, he's got his whatever—and when he brings about the result, he's doing it. He is the one who pulls it off. But the priest never says, look what I'm going to do; I'm going to heal you. No. The priest is the intermediary between the god and the person in the church. So I think that another distinction is, magic is more immediate. The magician is saying, I'm doing it. Whereas the priest or religious person, it's the gods doing it. So always in religion we have gods. Whereas in magic we don't necessarily have gods.

Now the Egyptians, of course, were up to the neck in magic. They did magic and religion. And it's harder for them to make that distinction between magic and religion. Let me give you an example that will sort of almost argue against what I've said. But I think what I've said is right. The Egyptians had a goddess of magic. Now, I've just said the magician does it on his own. But somehow, there is a goddess of magic. Heka was her name. Usually, by the way, the gods who were associated with magic are women. Heka is the goddess of magic. There's also Isis, who had tremendous powers, if you'll remember. She raises Osiris from the dead, even. And she has the title "She Who Knows Everyone's Name." And the idea was that, if you knew a person's name, you could work magic against him. So the ultimate is if you know everyone's name you got it. There's even a story of how Isis got her power over the god Re, where the god Re was sick. He was dying. And she was going to help him. But she said, "Tell me your name." And he gives her a name. But that's not his—she tries the magic, it doesn't work. It's not his real name.

Egyptians if you remember, often had two names. One was the name by which everybody knew him, for example, Imhotep. But then there was your real name, which only your mother knew. Because then if somebody tried to do a magical spell on you, and they used Imhotep, but that's not your real name, your real name is Harry, then the magic wouldn't work. So there was a secret name. So Isis learns the secret name of Re, and thereby gets power over him. So her name is "She Who Knows Every One's Name." Power is in knowing the name so you could say the words.

So there are goddesses and gods associated with magic. But I think there is this distinction that the magician is really pulling it off. And I think in religion it's an intermediary. But let's see what the parts of a magical outcome involve.

First there's the spell. Words that are spoken. And let me emphasize, and I think this is important. There's a tendency to think that magic is just any mumbo jumbo that any magician wants to say. No. There were basic principles of magic. In the same way, you may not believe in astrology today. You may not believe in astrology. But certainly there is a right and a wrong way to do astrology. Correct ways to draw charts. Correct ways to plot the heavens. It may not be efficacious, it may not work. But there's a right and a wrong way. There's a logic to it. And it's the same with magic. So in magic, one of the basic principles is the word is the deed. In other words if you say it—under the right conditions—it will become so. If I say "Oh, may I live forever" it might happen if I say it under the right conditions. So the word is the deed is a basic principle, and that's why the spell is so important.

Next element of magic. The ritual. It's a little bit like theater. There is some performance involved in magic that makes it work. Sometimes for example, sometimes it might be drawing the protective circle on the ground. Remember, the pharaoh's name is written in a cartouche? That oval? That magically encircles his name. Encircling was very important—crucial concept to the Egyptians. And for example a magical spell to make sure—Now, remember, scorpions were a real fear in ancient Egypt. There were plenty of scorpions. And there are today. I mean, if you stay in some of the smaller rest houses on the west bank of the Nile, everybody knows the first thing you do is, you dump your shoes out upside down to make sure if there's any scorpion crawled in there it gets out. And also, if you're going into a tomb that people haven't been in in a while, you get that flashlight and you look for scorpions. So scorpions were a real problem. And there were spells to make sure that you wouldn't be bitten at night as you slept. And what did you do?

Well there is a spell, you say "oh scorpion, bite not me," that kind of thing. But important is you took, or the magician took his wand. And there were magical wands in ancient Egypt. Plenty of them. We still have them. They're kind of in the shape and about the size of a large boomerang. That's how they worked in ancient Egypt. And they were usually made of bone or ivory and had magical carvings on them. And if you wanted to make sure that this spell worked against scorpions, the magician would take his wand, and as he's reciting this spell, he would draw around your bed in the dirt. So you'd have a circle protecting you. So that's a kind of ritual.

Next the magician. He's the third element. You can't just find a magician's wand and necessarily make it work. You can't just say the words. The magician has to be a special person. In a sense he's a hero. He is controlling the forces of nature. Now often magicians came from temples, and this is where it gets hard to separate a magician from a priest. Often magicians were indeed priests also. But somehow it seemed like they could do magic also, rather than just asking the gods.

For example, if you'll remember in the Old Testament, when Pharaoh calls for his magicians, the word that is used remember in Coptic—the late form of Egyptian—and in the Coptic Bible, which still exists today, is *sesperonch*. That's the word for magician in Coptic. Now what does that mean? *Ses* is "scribe," *per* is "house," and *onch* is "life." These were "scribes of the House of Life." These were priests who were sort of schooled in this kind of thing, in the House of Life, which was a school associated with the temple. Even today, we have the tradition in Egypt of there being schools attached to temples. To mosques. They're called "madrassas." Next to the mosque is a place of learning. So the magician was a special person. Sometimes a priest. But sometimes he was a layman. I think very often in the rural areas, where there were no large temples, no books available to look up things, then I think you have laymen filling in this role. And these were like in a sense the country doctors who did everything, and even one further removed, we just had a midwife who did everything. These were the magicians who sort of made it up as they went along. Maybe not really schooled that well, but they could do it.

So you have three basic elements in any magical performance. You have the spell—the words spoken. You have the ritual—some performance. And you have the magician—some special person. Now magical practices differed considerably, depending upon the outcome desired. Let me tell you about one element of magic that is so common to Egyptologists. We find these things all the time, and they're just wonderful little things. They're magical servant statues. You'll remember of course, that the Egyptians were resurrectionists. They believed that in the next world, they were literally going to get up and go again and work. Now they viewed the next world as a continuation of this one. It was going to be basically the same. So bring your tennis racquet, whatever, and you bring everything you could.

Now because Egypt was mainly agrarian, a farming country, they viewed the next world as a place where there's going to be a lot of farming. They were going to be in the Elysian Fields, so to speak. There were going to be fields where you farmed. And if you look on tomb walls, you very often see these scenes of people farming in the fields of the next world. And it was very much like this world. There's a plow, there might be an oxen pulling the plow. But you know, the people are always dressed up in their finest linens. It's kind of like, it's going to be like this world, but it's air conditioned. You get that feeling that it's kind of like, it's better. Believe me.

Now Egypt, as you know, had a strong centralized government, which is what it made it great right from the time of Narmer. And one of the things that made Egypt great, was they could focus all their manpower on irrigation canals. They could bring the Nile water in and irrigate more land than you might expect. And this was a kind of communal work project. When inundation came, they had to have those irrigation channels ready. And the pharaoh could say, the astronomer priest would say, "Well, it's July. The Nile is going to rise very soon. We'd better get these canals ready." And they would call upon the population of Egypt—all the farmers—and put them where they were needed. You're going to dig this canal. You're going over there. You're going over there. It was kind of by fiat. And I think the ancient Egyptians, when they thought about the next world, figured that this was going to happen in the next world. They were going to be called upon to do farm labor. But the next world was going to be better.

How? Servant statues. You could have statues made and placed in your tomb. And these statues are called *ushabtis*. It's an ancient Egyptian word. And it means "answerer," from the verb *wesheb*, "to answer." "W" and "u" are the same, so it's *wesheb* or *usheb*. *Ushabtis*—meaning "I'm answering." These little statues—when you were called in the next world to do work, these little statues would say, "Here I am!" And it would get up and work for you.

Now many, many Egyptians were buried with 365 of these statues— one for each day of the year. They were sort of like union shops. They say, only work one day a year. And they would work when called. And they are lovely little figures. And the kind of statues you had depended upon what you could afford. Some of them are beautiful works of art, made out of *faïence*, which is a quartzite paste—a paste, remember, that is fired in a kiln and glazes itself. So it can be green or blue. And they're rather beautiful. And usually, the *ushabti*—the little figure, the little servant statue—has two or three characteristics that you know right away, ah, this is a servant statue. One is, the legs are together. It's a standing figure. Because he's wrapped like a mummy. It's associated with Osiris, because it's going to be in the Land of the Dead. But also, the hands are crossed across the chest. And in the hands are farm implements. These guys are going to work in the next world.

Sometimes, on *ushabtis* that are very, very carefully done, over the back of the shoulder is a seed pack. You can see, it's a little straw pack, slung over the shoulder, that these guys are going to go through the fields and throw out the seeds in the next world. So these *ushabti* statues are everywhere. And 365, if you were really wealthy. Tutankhamen had more than 400. And every one was an individual, beautiful portrait of Tutankhamen, the face. They're spectacular.

Let me tell you a little detail. A kind of almost Disney trivia. But it's really Egyptological trivia about—do you know where, in a Walt Disney film, you see *ushabtis*? The very first movie I ever saw was "Fantasia." Now, I don't know if you remember "Fantasia." It's the one where—it's a cartoon of course, and there's a sequence in "Fantasia." Mostly fantastic things happen in "Fantasia." That's why it's called that. But there's a sequence called "The Sorcerer's Apprentice," where Mickey Mouse has a sorcerer's hat on, and kind of a sorcerer-type cloak. And he teaches a broomstick to fetch water. And if you remember, it gets out of hand. The broomstick won't stop fetching the water. And he takes an axe and slices the broomstick in half, and now you've got two of them fetching water. That is an ancient Egyptian story. That is from an ancient Egyptian papyrus about a magician who tries to train a broomstick to do this. It's pure Egyptian. Pure Egyptian.

Also on every *ushabti* statue, if you were wealthy, if you had a big enough one that could hold an inscription, is a magical spell. And it's part of the "Book of the Dead." Because if you couldn't afford *ushabtis*, you could maybe have a piece of paper that would do it. Hopefully. It's a spell from the "Book of the Dead" which says basically, if I am called to do work in the next world, answer, "here I am." If I am called to haul sand from the east to the west, do my bidding. If I am called to work in the fields, answer, "here I am." And then the name of the deceased. So the *ushabtis* would know, oh, your name is Amenhotep. So if I hear "Amenhotep" at the corvée, when the people are called to work, I will pop up and do the work. So these *ushabti* statues became a central part of Egyptian culture. There were whole factories that made these, cranking them out of molds.

And you know what's neat? I mean, they really thought the next world was going to be like this one. For every 10 *ushabtis* you had, you had an overseer *ushabti* to make sure they worked. And the overseer *ushabti*, you can tell, is different. He has a starched kilt on. And the starched kilt was a sign that, I don't have to do manual labor. I mean with that starched kilt you can't do anything, you can't move around. It's—like a mini-skirt practically. And the idea is, to make sure that these 10 guys do it, you've got an overseer for each 10. And when you went to your tomb, they were packed very neatly in boxes—little *ushabti* boxes. So this is a bit of magic that everybody wanted.

If you were real poor, you couldn't afford these big beautiful faïence *ushabti* statues. No. They would be made out of perhaps terracotta. And somebody in your house—maybe somebody who's taking an art class, so to speak, you know an amateur artist, would fashion these little things. And sometimes they looked practically like crude cigarettes, they looked so poorly done. But you would be buried with these in the hope that they would serve you in the next world. So this is only one little facet of magic. But it became a major industry in ancient Egypt. And essential regalia for the next world.

Now there were also statues that were called "oracle statues." and these are really interesting things. Now they were statues of the gods, but these statues could supposedly talk. Now, we've never found one that we think is an oracle statue. But you know, what you might think is—for example, like they're a little bit like maybe a mannequin, almost. A puppet, where the jaw might drop open and close. We never found anything like that. But these oracle statues were central to the culture. Again there is actually a papyrus that records the case of an oracle statue who solved a crime. Some watchman was sleeping on the job at the warehouse. And some shirts were stolen while he was sleeping. And the question was, who took it?

Now when you went to court in ancient Egypt, you could do two things. You could go before real people—a court, with judges. Now the judges were usually, by the way, elders of the village. There were no lawyers in ancient Egypt. There was no concept that you needed somebody to speak for yourself. You presented your case. The other side presented its case. And the elders would decide. But if you didn't want to take that route—sort of, I guess, traditional judicial route—you could go to an oracle statue. And its decision was binding. And this watchman, who thought he knew who stole his shirts, went before an oracle. And we're told he said, "So and so stole the shirts." And the other guy came and he said, "I didn't steal the shirts." And the oracle nodded or indicated in some way, this guy did steal the shirts. Now you're allowed a second hearing—you could appeal. And they went to another oracle statue. And this watchman who had slept on the job started reading the names of the people in the village. And when he got to the name of this guy he had accused, the oracle indicated, "Yep, that's the guy." And this guy was convicted. So oracle statues could in some way speak. And they have legal weight. Quite interesting.

But I think the bit of magic that dominates Egyptian life more than anything are amulets, magical amulets. This was something everybody could afford. Now let me define for you what an amulet is. It is a small object worn for protection. That, by the way, is the ancient Egyptian etymology of the word. Originally, these things were called things like "protectors." And there were many amulets. Different amulets for different goals intended. For example, the Eye of Horus. Now the Eye of Horus was, I think, one of the most popular of all amulets. It was a small thing. Worn around the neck usually. You know, maybe an inch or so. And it represented the eye of the falcon god Horus. Now why was that such an important magical amulet? If you'll remember, Horus did battle with Seth, his evil uncle. And he tried—he tried—to kill him, but he didn't. But he beats him up. But in the battle, Horus's eye is taken out. Now the eye was magically regenerated by the god Toth, god of writing, also the god of magic. So the eye is magically regenerated and it became the sign of health. And it represents the very sort of characteristic markings of a falcon's eye.

If you look in a museum—more than anyplace, a natural history museum—at a falcon, you'll see the parts of the eye are really carefully reproduced in this magical amulet. And I'll tell you something that we get today, that people do not realize, from the Eye of Horus. A symbol that every one of you knows that became a sign of health. The pharmacist's "Rx," as in, prescription. The pharmacist's "Rx" is really a corruption of part of the Eye of Horus, part of the elements of the Eye of Horus. Now if you know Latin, Rx doesn't mean anything. It doesn't mean anything. The Eye of Horus, in the Middle Ages, became a kind of sign of health, and that that was corrupted eventually by the apothecaries to be the "Rx." So the Eye of Horus becomes our symbol of health also. So if you wanted to be healthy, the Eye of Horus was worn. And if you'll remember last time, we were talking about the grave robbers. And that they took the Eye of Horus amulets from the bodies of the kings. These were things that were worn both by the living and by the deceased.

Now, the most common of all magical amulets was the scarab. That was the one—we find literally thousands of them. Thousands. That, and the Eye of Horus, are the two that we find all the time. Now, the scarab is a carved beetle, it's carved in the shape of a beetle. And remember I mentioned it once before. The word for beetle was a pun. In ancient Egyptian it was pronounced "kheper." That meant two things. One, it meant "beetle." But the other meant "to exist." So if you wore a beetle around your neck, you would exist. It was for continuing existence. So that's an important one.

One other thing about the scarab, by the way, why the Egyptians were so interested in scarabs and beetles. It had to do with a little bit of bad biology. Egyptians weren't great on biology really by any means. They believed that the scarab procreated without a male and female. They thought that there was only a female, or maybe only a male. The reason is, they saw the scarab—the beetle, the actual beetle. It's a dung beetle. And it's called *scarabeus sacre*. That's the Latin name. And that's where we get scarab, from *scarabeus sacre*, "the sacred scarab." The sacred beetle. They saw scarabs pushing their dung balls in front of them. Now, the female lays the eggs in a dung ball so that it will have, they'll have food when they hatch—the eggs of the young. And they saw them pushing this thing and it looked like the sun, this large disk being rolled across the horizon. And because they thought there wasn't a male and female—and they never caught them at it—because they thought it was male and female, they thought this was a very special animal. So the scarab became sacred. So scarabs are another thing the Egyptians loved to wear. They also used them as signet rings. On the bottom of the scarab, the flat part, you would carve your name and you could seal your wine jar. So the servants couldn't get into it. Put a little clay at the top and seal it. So another important aspect were these magical amulets.

Another one, that I think is really surprising, is the magical amulet that everybody knows about today. People wear them, I see people wearing them all the time. The *ankh*—the cross, the Egyptian cross. That means life. It's a loop on top, and then the regular cross. Two arms going across and down. The surprising thing is the *ankh* is perhaps the rarest of all amulets. We never find them. You never find them in excavations. We always see gods painted on temples holding them and touching it to the nose of the pharaoh, giving him life. But I think this may have been something reserved to the gods. Because it's very rare. Very rare as an amulet.

Now another one is solely for the dead. As I mentioned, some are for the living, some are for the dead. Another one is called the *djed* pillar. This is a little amulet usually. And it's carved. It looks like a pillar. It looks like a pillar with some lines across it. And what it represents is the backbone of the god Osiris. And if you wore this, you'd have stability, because the backbone is what gives you stability. The lines across—I think really represent vertebrae going across.

Now for amulets though it wasn't just the shape. No. The material you made the amulet out of was important. That had magical properties also. For example, the backbone of Osiris, the *djed* pillar. It was best if it was carved out of bone, because Osiris's real backbone was bone of course. So the idea is that, as close as you can come to the association, make it look like the backbone, make it out of the same material, then maybe it'll work.

Also important for many of these amulets is color. I think very often, for the Egyptians, very often that they were just as interested in the color as the material. For example, sometimes red would represent blood. And the "knot of Isis," a knot that she used to tie her garment with, always had to be red. Something to do with blood. So it's not just the amulet itself, it's the color. And the material. But magic was just absolutely essential to the ancient Egyptian worldview. Crucial. Now, with this detour away from chronological history, next time we'll go back and we'll try to trace the history of Egypt, which we saw was slipping away. I'll see you then.

Lecture Thirty-Six
Dynasty XXI—Egypt Divided

Scope:

In Lecture Thirty-Four, we saw Egypt slip to the point at which Heri-Hor, the High Priest of Amun, wrote his name in a cartouche and ruled as pharaoh in Thebes. In Dynasty XXI, we will see Egypt's long slide continue into two simultaneous dynasties—one in Thebes and one in the Delta. The descendants of Heri-Hor rule in Thebes, while in the Delta, the "official kings" rule. Egyptian history has become a tale of two cities. But there is more in them of peaceful coexistence than a state of war.

Outline

I. Priest kings ruled from Thebes (1080–945 B.C.).

    A. Heri-Hor (1080–1074 B.C.) died before Ramses XI, but he set the stage for other priest kings.

    B. Piankh (1074–1070 B.C.) was both king and high priest of Amun. He died around the same time as Ramses XI.

    C. Pinedjem I (1070–1032 B.C.) married the daughter of Ramses XI (Henetowey I), so these are not warring factions.

        1. He inspected the Valley of the Kings and restored damaged mummies. This was a sign that Egypt was weak and couldn't protect the royal necropolis.

        2. Egyptians dated years according to who was king—a "pharaoh-centric" calendar. Pinedjem dated his reign as during the rule of Smendes I, the real king, in the Delta—another sign of peaceful coexistence.

        3. When Pinedjem's *ushabtis* began appearing on the antiquities market in the 1870s, the search for a royal tomb began in earnest. The *ushabtis* still occasionally appear on the market.

    D. Masaherta (1054–1046 B.C.) was Pinedjem's son and High Priest of Amun but wasn't very important.

    E. Menkheperre (1045–992 B.C.) was another son of Pinedjem and also a High Priest of Amun. The pattern had been set.

    F. Smendes II (992–990 B.C.) was a son of Menkheperre.

G. Pinedjem II (990–969 B.C.) was another son of Menkheperre.

  1. He carried out an inspection of the royal tombs and found that virtually all of them had been robbed. He brought the royal bodies together for safety away from the Valley of the Kings.

  2. His burial was found intact in the same royal cache, probably his original burial place.

H. Of Psusennes "III" (969–945 B.C.), nothing is known; his name appears in many different forms because a consistent transliteration for it is lacking. This is the last of the high priests ruling out of Thebes.

II. The kings of Tanis (1069–945 B.C.) ruled from the Delta in the north. These were the "official" kings.

  A. Smendes I (1069–1043 B.C.) declared himself king after the death of Ramses XI.

  1. He moved the capital from Piramesse to Tanis. Many of Ramses II's works (statues, obelisks) were transferred with him.

  2. This caused early excavators to think Tanis was Piramesse.

  B. Amenemnisu (1043–1039 B.C.) was the son of Heri-Hor, the high priest of Thebes, another sign that Thebes and Tanis were cooperating.

  C. Psusennes I (1039–991 B.C.) was the longest reigning king of this dynasty.

  1. His intact tomb was discovered, rivaling even Tutankhamen's.

  2. He had been buried in the sarcophagus of Merneptah in nested coffins. He also had his own silver coffin with a gold mask. They were not poor!

  D. Another cache of royal mummies was preserved by these Theban priest-kings of Dynasty XXI. In 1898, Victor Loret discovered the tomb of Amenhotep II, a discovery that would eventually lead to Loret's having a nervous breakdown.

  1. The tomb had been plundered in antiquity. But in a side room, Loret found the mummies of an old woman, a prince, and a young woman. Because they all had holes in their heads, he began to wonder if he had found a case of human sacrifice.

2. In another sealed-off side-chamber he found the biggest surprise: nine more mummies in coffins.

3. Loret had found another royal cache, similar to the one at Deir el Bahri. Here were the mummies of Amenhotep III, Merneptah, and seven others!

4. This explains how Psusennes came to be buried with the lid of Merneptah's sarcophagus. The latter's body had been moved to the tomb of Amenhotep II for safe-keeping, but not the huge sarcophagus. Instead, it was shipped north to Tanis.

E. Amenemope (993–984 B.C.) was the son of Psusennes I. Buried at Tanis in his mother's tomb, next to his father's, he too had a gold face mask.

F. Osorkon the Elder (984–978 B.C.) is a puzzle. Not much is known about him.

G. Siamum (978–959 B.C.) seems to have been quite active.

1. He built extensively at the Temple of Amun (god of Thebes) at Tanis.

2. He rewrapped several royal mummies at Thebes, showing concern for tradition.

3. There is a Biblical connection with Siamum. This is the period when David fought the Philistines and united the tribes of Israel. David's son, Solomon, married an Egyptian princess, thought to be a daughter of Siamum; now Egypt's princesses were "marrying out."

H. Psusennes II (959–945 B.C.) ended the dynasty.

III. There is an interesting consequence of these kings of Dynasty XXI, who hid the bodies of their ancestors in places no one could have predicted.

A. When Victor Loret first entered the tomb of Amenhotep II, he found three mummies. An Egyptologist noticed that the left arm of one of them—"the elder lady"—was placed across the chest in a position often reserved for royalty.

B. All three mummies were of the New Kingdom. But it was unclear who they might be.

C. Among the thousands of items found in Tutankhamen's tomb, it turned out, was a tiny mummy-shaped box with the name of Queen Tiye on it. Inside was a lock of hair, a keepsake from Tutankhamen's grandmother.

1. Because hair is chemically unique, it was decided to compare the hair in the box with that of the "elder lady."
2. With permission from the Egyptian government, Dr. James Harris, an expert on royal mummies, had them tested and concluded that they were a match.

Essential Reading:

Aidan Dodson, *Monarchs of the Nile*, Chapter XIV.

Supplementary Reading:

Peter A. Clayton, *Chronicle of the Pharaohs*, pp. 182–189.

Questions to Consider:

1. How did the priests become kings?
2. What are the signs of wealth of the kings of Tanis?

Lecture Thirty-Six—Transcript
Dynasty XXI—Egypt Divided

Welcome back. Remember last time we took a little bit of a side detour from our chronological history of Egypt, and we talked about ancient Egyptian magic. I'd like to go back two lessons before. And if you'll remember, we were talking about the XXth Dynasty. And at the end of that dynasty, something absolutely outrageous for Egyptian history occurred. The High Priest of Amun at Thebes, a man named Heri-Hor, wrote his name in a cartouche indicating that he was king of Egypt. Not only that, he built his own temple at Karnak Temple, dedicated to Khonsu, the son of Amun and Mut. So he's building his own temple. And on the walls of that temple that he put up, on those walls he is shown the same size as the king of Egypt who is ruling in the north. So in a sense he's claiming, I'm king of Egypt also. There are two people claiming to be king of Egypt—one is Ramses XI in the north, and the other is our man Heri-Hor. It's outrageous.

Now how does this happen? Well the dynasty we're going to look at today, the XI^h Dynasty, is unique. It's in a sense a tale of two cities. We have two simultaneous dynasties ruling. One from the north. And one from the south. We have the descendents of Heri-Hor, this high priest, calling themselves kings, ruling from Thebes. And in the North, we have a totally separate dynasty, also calling themselves kings. That's why I say it's a tale of two cities. Now many Egyptologists might think, and do think, that what we've got really is warring factions. We've got kind of the Hatfields and the McCoys, slugging it out over who was king of Egypt. I'm king. You're king. You know. That kind of thing. No, I don't think so. I think really we have a kind of peaceful co-existence. I want you to bear with me and try to play detective a little bit. What I'd like you to do is, as I describe what happens during this dynasty—actually two dynasties, one in the north and one in the south—I'd like you to look for signs that there's really a peaceful co-existence. Let's try it.

I'm going to start first with the priest kings of the south. These people are all high priests of Amun, and they are ruling from Thebes. And let's talk about what they do and what their reign is like. Now as I mentioned, the one who starts this whole thing is Heri-Hor, the high priest who builds his little temple there and depicts himself as large as the king, puts his name in a cartouche. Well, he dies before

Ramses XI, who was ruling in the north. He is succeeded by another High Priest of Amun—Piankh. And Piankh dies about the same time as Ramses XI, just about. But the important thing is in the south, in Thebes, we have a pattern established. The high priest will take over and call himself king.

Now, the next high hriest who rules in Thebes is Pinedjem. And he is important. He does things. Now first, how does he become high priest? Well, that's hereditary. You didn't have to have a special religious calling to be a priest. You just had to say the right words, do the deeds. So, he can do that easily enough. But how does he become king? Well if you'll remember there's a theory that you became pharaoh by marrying the right woman. The heiress theory—that there is a woman who carries in her royal blood the right to be king. So whom does he marry? He marries the daughter of Ramses XI, the king who had ruled in the north. Now it sounds to me as if these are not warring factions. But Pinedjem does other things, not just marrying a daughter.

He inspected the Valley of the Kings. Now, he's high priest. One of his jobs is to make sure that the religion remains intact. And he has an inspection of the Valley of the Kings, in which he discovers the tombs of the pharaohs have been plundered. Now remember, he's trying to be a king himself. So he is going to view these people as pharaohs and his ancestors, both. These are my people. He restores the mummies. He has some of them rewrapped, and he labels them. So he's trying to carry out what a pharaoh should do. Now, he dates his reign in a very interesting way. And here we're going to do a little side trip.

I want to explain how the Egyptians kept track of their years, because Pinedjem does something very important for us. We keep years consecutively. After the year 2000, we know what year is coming, 2001, and after that, 2002, and so on. We have a nice long consecutive string. The Egyptians did not do that. And that's why sometimes it's hard for us to figure out, in what year did this happen? The pharaoh was so central to the Egyptian mentality that their calendar depended on who was king. It was kind of a pharaoh-centric calendar. So for example, when a pharaoh like Ramses the Great died, during his reign he would have kept count of the years of his reign. First year of Ramses the Great. Second year of Ramses the Great. His last year would be the 67th year of Ramses the Great. And if an event took place during that reign, he'd say month three, day one of the year of Ramses 67. But what happened when Ramses died? Well, the next year is not year 68. No. The new king, and in this case remember? The 13th son of Ramses became pharaoh, Merneptah—the next year is year one of Merneptah. So the Egyptians kept track of their days, months, years in terms of pharaoh's reigns.

Now remember Pinedjem, our high priest, has married the daughter of Ramses XI, and he's claiming he's king. He's looked in the Valley of the Kings, he's tidied it up, he's preserved the bodies. How does he keep track of the years of his reign? He doesn't say year one of Pinedjem. Year two of Pinedjem. No. He dates his years according to the king who was ruling in the north. Somebody who's now replaced Ramses XI—Smendes. So he says, year one of Smendes, year two of Smendes. In other words, this is a sign of deference to the kings of the north. That they're really the kings. I'm calling myself king, but I'll keep track by their years. So I think this is another sign that we really don't have a kind of warring faction. There is a peaceful co-existence. They're managing it with each other.

Now there is a kind of neat little sidebar about Pinedjem's *ushabti* statues. Remember last time when we talked about Egyptian magic, I mentioned that if you were wealthy enough, you wanted 365 *ushabtis*—one for each day of the year. They were going to serve you in the next world. Well, Pinedjem's *ushabtis* are the ones that started the search for that royal tomb that had been discovered by tomb robbers, that led to finding all the royal mummies together. You'll remember that in the 1870s, antiquities started appearing on the market that were from a royal tomb. And immediately the antiquities service knew a royal tomb has been found, and we have to find it. Well, the whole thing that started it was Pinedjem's little *ushabti* statutes—these bright blue things. They were being sold. And somebody knew his tomb had been found. Interestingly, by the way you can still see these *ushabtis* on the market today. They appear in the auction houses. You know like Sotheby's and Christie's, these upscale places. And every once in a while, you see one of Pinedjem's *ushabtis* for sale. And you know that these were found by the tomb robbers in the 1870s, 1880s, sold on the market, and they're still knocking around. It's a bit of history.

But Pinedjem dies. And he's succeeded by two of his sons. Remember the high priest is a hereditary thing. You can do it. One is not important. Masaherta. Not very important. Menkheperre is another High Priest of Amun. But the pattern has been set. These guys don't reign that long. But we have high priests ruling as kings. Now Menkheperre's successors are two of his sons. One, Smendes II. Minor. Reigns a few years. But the next, Pinedjem II—interesting things happen.

Now first, he carries out another inspection of the royal necropolis. the Valley of the Kings. He finds that virtually all of the tombs have been robbed. But he makes a decision. Kind of executive thinking. Also, it indicates the state of Egypt. He realizes the Valley of the Kings cannot be protected anymore. He's given up on the Valley of the Kings and all hope that you can put a guard there, or anything like that. Things have deteriorated so much in Egypt that he's got to move the mummies. Move them. He is the one who gathers together many of these mummies, and has them moved to a secret cliff tomb at Deir el Bahri. And he thinks that this tomb is so safe that he will choose it as his final burying place. And it is safe. It remains safe for more than 3,000 years. So this is the place his burial is found in this tomb. But he realizes. it's over for Egypt. We can't protect the Valley of the Kings. And no longer will the pharaohs be buried in the Valley of the Kings. So remember, not all pharaohs are buried in pyramids—that's way earlier in the history of Egypt. And not all pharaohs are buried in the Valley of the Kings. Different places for different times.

So anyway Pinedjem II dies, is buried in his safe tomb. And he's succeeded by a very minor king—Psusennes. Let me say something about the name Psusennes, Psusennes III, he's called—names are unfortunately not consistent in Egyptology. You might say Psusennes. You might hear Psusennes. You might hear Psusenes. You might hear Psaneus—same guy. We don't have a consistent transliteration for it. We should, we really should, but we don't. But with him, with this minor pharaoh, it's the end—it's the end of these high priests ruling out of Thebes.

Now remember, while they're ruling, we have the kings in the north who are also kings of Egypt, probably the official kings. And let's talk about that consecutive dynasty that's running along also. Now first remember we had Ramses XI. Well, Ramses XI dies, as we know. Smendes takes over—Who? Who's Smendes? We don't really know. He's declares himself king. If I had to bet, I'd say the reason he could declare himself king is military. He's a military man. Remember back to the time of Tutankhamen, for example, when there were turbulent times. And after Tutankhamen we had a vizier ruling, Aye, for a little while. But then, there's no children, there's no clear successor. Who takes over? Horemheb. The general. Almost always, in hard times, the military takes over. I mean it's the same in South America. That happens today. So probably, if I had to bet, a military man who declares himself king.

Now what does he do? First, he moves the capital. He moves the capital from that biblical city that Ramses created Pi-Ramses to another site in the in the Delta, this marshy area almost, Tanis. Now he causes a problem for archaeologists with this move. When he moves, he takes with them the large statues of Ramses the Great that Ramses had built for his biblical city. He takes with them the obelisks. They're small obelisks, but they're obelisks that Ramses had erected there. And he brings them to his new capital, because he wants to show, "we're grand." But he may not be able to build everything so quickly. So this is kind of like a ready-made, pre-fabricated city—you know, you take an obelisk, you take a statue, and you've got it.

Now the problem is, later archaeologists, when they excavated at the new site, Tanis, they found all these statues of Ramses. And they figured, "Ah, this is the biblical city of Ramses!" I mean it's perfectly reasonable to think. You find all these status of Ramses, Ramses put them here. But no. They were moved. So Smendes moves the capital.

Anyway, when he dies, he is followed by a pharaoh named Amenemnisu. The name isn't important. What's really important is, whose son is he? Heri-Hor's. Remember that name? That was the high priest of Thebes who started it all in the south by writing his name in a cartouche. So we've got a son of Heri-Hor now, sort of being shuffled north to become king. And I think this shows that Thebes in the south and this new dynasty at Tanis in the north are cooperating. They're sort of shifting people. Now he is followed by Psusennes I.

I will tell you something that's going to tantalize you. I promise I will give you the full details in the next lecture, but let me say this.

The tomb of this king, Psusennes I, was found intact. It rivaled Tutankhamen's. I will explain why you don't know about it next time. I promise. But let me tell you something about the burial, just the burial of his—I'll give you the details of the discovery of the tomb later. Let me say what he was buried in, first of all. He's buried at Tanis. His new capital. He was buried in a pink Aswan granite—big pink Aswan granite sarcophagus. The lid to that sarcophagus was Merneptah's. Merneptah, the 13th son who became king. The 13th son of Ramses the Great who became king. It's kind of curious.

Now think about this. Merneptah was buried in the Valley of the Kings. What is this Tanite king, coming later, doing with Merneptah's lid to his sarcophagus? Now, I'll complete the description of his burial and then I'll tell you how I think he got it, how he got that lid. Inside that sarcophagus with Merneptah's lid, was another stone sarcophagus—black granite. Inside that was another alabaster one. Inside that was a solid silver coffin. Solid silver. Now let me say this. Silver, if you'll remember, was more valuable than gold in Egypt—about three times. These kings of Tanis were not poor. Everybody makes a big deal out of Tutankhamen's gold coffin. This is three times as valuable. It's silver. And beautiful. Inside that silver coffin was the body of the pharaoh, badly damaged Tanis is a moist area. It was basically a skeleton. And even around the bones were some aquatic plants. You know, some kind of vines growing around. Really quite something. But the face of the pharaoh, the skull, was covered with a gold mask. Not un-like Tutankhamen this burial. Wealthy. These people were not poor. That's the important thing.

Now I promised I'd tell you, how did he wind up with Merneptah's sarcophagus lid? Well remember the Deir el Bahri cache, when all the mummies were brought together by the high priest and moved for safety. That was not the only time that happened. Not the only time that royal mummies came together to be moved. There was another time. And this was another discovery of royal mummies. And let me tell you about this. The excavator was Victor Loret. Now Loret was a strange man—strange. He was made Director of Antiquities because the previous director resigned suddenly, Gaston Maspero, to go back to Paris. And Loret was the man who was there. He was quickly promoted, and he was a little bit above his head. He was a good archaeologist. And he decided to investigate the Valley of the Kings. This is 1898.

Now he was very impressionable—a kind word. Some people say he was unstable. The discovery that I'm going to tell you about literally led to him having a nervous breakdown—he had a nervous breakdown. As I say he was excavating in the Valley of the Kings. And in 1891 he found the tomb of the pharaoh, Amenhotep II. Much plundered. Understand, he is unprepared for what he is going to find. It was totally unsuspected. And he enters, and it's been plundered. But what does he see? He's going by candlelight. Now remember, there's no electricity in these tombs. And they turn. And in a side room, he finds three mummies lying on their backs. There's a mummy of an old woman, a mummy of a young prince. He has a side lock of youth on his hair. And there's a young woman. Now all three—their heads have been smashed in. There are holes in their heads. And Loret's mind is racing. He's thinking about human sacrifice. He's thinking about what has happened. I mean, what he doesn't realize is the tomb has been robbed, the robbers have used their axes to take the bandages off smashing through their heads. But he doesn't realize this yet, and he's got a long night ahead of him.

He then goes deeper in to the tomb. He finds the stone sarcophagus of Amenhotep II. And there, in the sarcophagus, is Amenhotep II. A plundered mummy, barely in rags, but it's a royal mummy. He continues. There's the mummy of a young man that's in a model boat that was supposed to take the pharaoh maybe to the next world, or be used in the next world.

But then he goes to another side chamber. And the side chamber is bricked up with stones during the time of the XXIst Dynasty kings. Now he takes down some of the bricks. Peers in. What does he see? Coffins. Nine of them. He removes the stones. He goes inside. Climbs over some of them. And he blows away the dust on one of them. And he can read a cartouche. It says "Ramses." And he's probably not sure which Ramses yet. Is it Ramses V? Is it Ramses VI? But it's a Ramses. It's a royal. And he wonders is this like Deir el Bahri? Have I found another royal cache of mummies? And he starts blowing the dust off of other mummies. And there are cartouches everywhere. He has found, indeed, another royal cache.

Now, in this royal cache is Amenhotep III. Remember the great dazzling king of the sun disk? Amenhotep III, one of Egypt's greatest. Also in this cache is the mummy of Ramses the Great's 13th son, Merneptah, who became king of Egypt. Now, remember

©1999 The Teaching Company.

I'm telling you this story to explain how a king in Tanis gets the lid of Merneptah. What I think happens is the following. When the high priests are doing these inventories of the Valley of the Kings, of course they discover the tombs have been plundered. What do they do? They're moving the mummies to safe places. One place is that Deir el Bahri cache high up in the cliff. Another is the tomb of Amenhotep II. They're going to put them all sort of—so to speak, they're going to put all their eggs in one basket. Put all the royal pharaohs in this side chamber, brick it up, and hope you can protect that one. And it worked. They stayed protected. Now, as you're bringing the pharaohs out of their original tombs, let's take Merneptah. He's buried in this huge sarcophagus. Pink Aswan granite. They're not going to drag that to the tomb of Amenhotep II. Everybody will see. It might be too crowded for it, it's only a small side room with nine mummies. So they leave it. They leave the sarcophagus behind. And they bury the mummy of Merneptah. Now, you've got this really neat sarcophagus and lid. Well, why should it go to waste? It's shipped north to Tanis for Psusennes to be buried in, and that's how a king in Tanis comes to be buried with the lid of a pharaoh buried in the Valley of the Kings. I think it's a cooperation between the people in the south in Thebes, who were overlooking, overseeing the Valley of the Kings, and the kings who were ruling in the north. But it's quite a burial, Psusennes's.

But anyway, these kings were not poor. His son, Amenemope, he was buried at Tanis also. He too had a gold face mask. A beautiful gold face mask. There are other kings of this dynasty. There's Osorkon the Elder. Hardly anything is known about him. But then we get Siamun. Siamun is interesting. He builds at Tanis, a sign that he's got some money. Wealth. Builds a temple. To whom? Amun. The principal god of Thebes. What you're really getting, in a sense, is Tanis is mirroring the religious capital at Thebes. Because the chief god in Thebes is Amun. And he's building a temple to Amun at Tanis. There seems to be a kind of almost mirror image of what's going on here.

Now, there's an interesting connection here with the Bible. With the Bible. Because during Siamun's reign we have a funny phenomenon. Now remember, this is the period when King David is fighting with the Philistines and he unites the tribes of Israel. This is a period when we start to get princesses of Egypt marrying out. Now, let me explain what I mean by marrying out. Remember in the good old days of

Ramses the Great when things were really good? Well Ramses married two Hittite princesses. He marries two of them, and this is a sign that the Hittite king wants to really be on the good side of Ramses, he's sending a beautiful daughter or two. And Ramses marries the daughters. Well for the first time—unheard of—we are getting kings of Egypt sending their daughters out. They are marrying foreigners. For example, in the Bible we have in Kings I, we've got a story. If you remember Hadad was an Edomite who flees to Egypt. And he becomes in with the pharaoh. He's one with the pharaoh. And what we're told is, Hadad became a great favorite of pharaoh. This is from the Bible. Hadad became a great favorite of pharaoh, who gave him his own wife's sister in marriage. The sister of the "Great Lady." Now "Great Lady" of course, is the translation of in Egyptian, *hemet weret*, "the great wife." So actually his queen's sister is given to an Edomite to marry. This is a big deal, because she is eventually going to leave the country with her husband. And to send an Egyptian out of the country was not at not an easy thing to do. David's son King Solomon marries an Egyptian princess.

So what we have here is a kind of almost reversal of power. It's like everybody wants to have a favorable trade balance. This is a reversal. We're getting Egypt's princesses going out of Egypt, whereas in the old days you had the foreign ones coming in for the king of Egypt to marry. Now the dynasty ends with Psusennes II, a minor king. Now what we've had are two dynasties I think peacefully co-existing. They exchange family members, they send a granite sarcophagus lid north, for one. It's not the warring Hatfields and McCoys that a lot of people think. But there's an interesting sidebar to what these— remember the high priests of Amun in the south? There's an interesting sidebar to one thing they did. And I want to tell you, because it's just a wonderful story. When they gathered together the bodies in the tomb of Amenhotep II, and remember Victor Loret when he was in there saw three bodies—an old lady, a prince with the side-lock of youth, and a young woman? Well they're unidentified. They'd been robbed. Any jewelry they had was taken off. Unidentified. Everybody thought they would remain unidentified forever. Maybe not. When these priests preserved these bodies, they may have really been preserving the grandmother of Tutankhamen. And let me tell you why I say that. The older woman, who became known as the "elder lady" around the Egyptian Museum in Cairo because she was an old lady, but nobody knew who she was. She was called the "elder lady." She had one arm, her left arm, placed across her chest. That is a sign of royalty. Usually royalty. And during the XVIIIth Dynasty also, it's a sign of royalty. An Egyptologist looked at this and said, you know, this woman's probably royal. That makes sense. It's a royal tomb. You have all these mummies of kings around. And the question then became, who's missing? Which royal lady, elder lady, would be missing? Now remember in this tomb was Merneptah. We know that. But also Amenhotep III. And his wife Queen Tiye is missing. Now is it possible that this woman is really Queen Tiye, who if you'll remember, would be the grandmother of Tutankhamen. She's the mother of Akhenaten, who is probably the father of Tutankhamen.

Is there any way we can prove that the "elder lady" is Queen Tiye? Well the answer is, probably. In Tutankhamen's tomb was a small coffinette, and it had on it the name of his grandmother, Queen Tiye. In the coffinette was a little gold statue, but also a lock of hair of Queen Tiye. A keepsake of grandma. Because he could keep that— he couldn't talk about his father, the heretic pharaoh, but he could keep grandma's hair. So there's a lock of Queen Tiye's hair.

Now, hair is very much like fingerprints. It's unique. In a sense, based on the principle "you are what you eat," the chemistry of everybody's hair is different. And it can be analyzed, and we can match hair samples. Is it possible that the hair on the "elder lady" matches the hair on the lock of hair from Tutankhamen's tomb? James Harris—he's an actually an orthodontist; not a full-scale Egyptologist, but a very good researcher—James Harris did a lot of x-raying of the pharaohs. His specialty was x-raying pharaohs. But he also wondered the same thing I'm suggesting, that the hair might match. And he got permission from the Egyptian government to take one hair from the "elder lady." One hair from the lock from Tutankhamen's tomb, and compare. His conclusion was that the hair matched. That spectra analysis showed that indeed it seems as if this hair matched. So because of these priest kings of the XXIst Dynasty, and their attempt to preserve the mummies of the royal families, we may have located the grandmother of Tutankhamen.

But next time, we'll pick up the story when Egypt becomes united. No more two kingdoms, one in the north, one in the south. We're going to get unification. But it's going to be by foreigners. I'll see you then.

Classical Egyptian Alphabet

Hieroglyph	Description	Sound
	vulture	a
	foot	b
	placenta	ch
	hand	d
	arm	e
	horned viper	f
	jar stand	g
	twisted flax	h
	reed leaf	i
	snake	j(dj)
	basket	k

Classical Egyptian Alphabet

Hieroglyph	Description	Sound
owl	owl	m
water	water	n
mat	mat	p
hill	hill	q
mouth	mouth	r
folded cloth	folded cloth	s
pool of water	pool of water	sh
loaf of bread	loaf of bread	t
tethering ring	tethering ring	tch
quail chick	quail chick	u / w
two reed leaves	two reed leaves	y
door bolt	door bolt	z

Timeline

500,000–3200 B.C. ....Prehistoric Period.

3100 B.C. ....Narmer and Unification of Egypt.

3050–2686 B.C. ....First Two Dynasties.

2686–2647 B.C. ....Zoser Builds Step Pyramid.

2613–2589 B.C. ....Sneferu Builds First True Pyramid.

2589–2566 B.C. ....The Great Pyramid Constructed.

2181–2049 B.C. ....First Intermediate Period.

2134–1782 B.C. ....The Middle Kingdom.

1782–1650 B.C. ....Second Intermediate Period.

c. 1570 B.C. ....Hyksos Expelled.

1498–1483 B.C. ....Hatshepsut Rules Egypt.

1386–1349 B.C. ....Amenhotep III; New Kingdom
at Peak.

1350–1334 B.C. ....Akhenaten and Amarna Revolution.

1334–1325 B.C. ....Tutankhamen's Reign.

1279–1212 B.C. ....Ramses the Great.

1080–945 B.C. ....Dynasty XXI—Priest Kings.

945–715 B.C. ....Libyans Rule Egypt.

747–664 B.C. ....Nubians Rule Egypt.

664–525 B.C. ....Assyrians Rule Egypt.

525–359 B.C. ....Persians Rule Egypt.

360–343 B.C. ....Nectanebo II, Last Egyptian Ruler.

343–332 B.C. ....Second Persian Period.

332 B.C. ....Alexander the Great
Conquers Egypt.

323–30 B.C. ....Greeks Rule Egypt.

30 B.C. ....Death of Cleopatra.

Glossary

archaising: An artistic or literary style that imitates techniques of the Old Kingdom.

ba: Part of the soul, usually represented as having the head of a man and the body of a bird.

ben-ben stone: The earliest form of the obelisk, worshipped in temples.

Book of the Dead: A collection of magical spells and prayers intended to help the deceased resurrect in the next world.

canopic jars: Four jars used to hold the internal organs removed at the time of mummification.

cartouche: An oval encircling the name of a king or queen.

cenotaph: A symbolic tomb in addition to the deceased's real place of burial.

Coptic: Christian art and religion as practiced in Egypt.

corbel: An inward stepping of the walls of a room toward the ceiling.

coregency: Two pharaohs ruling at the same time by agreement, usually father and son.

demotic: A later form of writing the Egyptian language used after the 7th century B.C. The word is from the Greek meaning *people*, because it was the secular form of writing, as opposed to hieroglyphs.

determinative hieroglyph: A hieroglyph placed at the end of a word to clarify its meaning.

faience: A ceramic material used for making amulets and tiles.

festival of Opet: A religious festival during which the statues of the gods Amun, Mut, and Khonsu were taken from Karnak Temple to Luxor Temple.

heb-sed festival: A ritual intended to be celebrated every 30 years by the pharaoh to ensure his rejuvenation.

hieratic: The cursive form of writing the Egyptian language derived from hieroglyphs.

hypostyle hall: A room of a temple with columns supporting a roof.

ka: Part of the deceased's soul that is thought of as a double.

kings list: An official list of the kings of Egypt, usually carved on a temple wall.

kiosk: A small, open structure made of stone, usually attached to a temple in honor of a god.

maat: Divine order; also, the Goddess of Truth.

mastaba: A bench-shaped structure above a tomb, especially during the Old Kingdom.

mummy: Any preserved cadaver.

natron: A naturally occurring mixture of sodium carbonate, sodium bicarbonate, and sodium chloride—used to dehydrate the body in mummification.

necrotome: A knife believed to have been used by embalmers ("death knife").

obelisk: A tall shaft of a single stone, usually pink granite. Obelisks were placed in pairs at the entrances to temples.

oracle: A person divinely inspired who foresees the future.

papyrus: Writing material made from the stalks of the papyrus plant.

pharaoh: The divine ruler of Egypt, associated with Horus, the falcon god.

pylon: A monumental gateway or entrance to a temple or palace.

registration: In art works, the practice of having different figures on different levels or registers.

relieving chambers: Small rooms designed to distribute the weight stresses of the pyramid above; also called "stress-relieving chambers."

resurrection: The belief that the body will get up and live again in the next world.

sarcophagus: A stone receptacle for preserving a mummy.

scarab: The sacred beetle. Often amulets were carved in this shape to ensure continued existence.

serekh: A schematic representation of a palace facade with a rectangle above it in which the king's Horus name was written.

sesperonch: A Coptic word for "magician" derived from the ancient Egyptian words "scribe of the house of life."

stela: A round-topped standing stone carved with an inscription.

Stretching the Cord: A ceremony performed at the beginning of the construction of a temple.

Ushabti: Small statues of servants intended to serve the deceased in the next world.

Bibliography

General History and Chronology

Aldred, Cyril. *The Egyptians*. London: Thames & Hudson, 1998. A concise overview by a noted Egyptologist.

Breasted, James Henry. *A History of Egypt*. New York: Scribner's, 1920. Amazingly, this is still one of the most readable histories of Egypt and is still mostly accurate.

Clayton, Peter. *Chronicle of the Pharaohs*. London: Thames and Hudson, 1994. A wonderful dynasty-by-dynasty illustrated history of Egypt.

Dodson, Aidan. *Monarchs of the Nile*. London: Rubicon Press, 1995. Brief descriptions of each pharaoh's reign. More a reference work than a readable history.

Gardiner, Alan. *Egypt of the Pharaohs*. Oxford: Oxford University Press, 1972. A dated work but by a great authority who gives many interesting details based on linguistic research. Not an easy read.

Hoffman, Michael A. *Egypt Before the Pharaohs*. New York: Knopf, 1979. The best book on prehistoric Egypt.

James, T. G. H. *An Introduction to Ancient Egypt*. New York: Farrar, Straus & Giraux, 1979. A concise and accurate history by the former Keeper of Egyptian Antiquities of the British Museum.

Mertz, Barbara. *Temples, Tombs, and Hieroglyphs*. New York: Dodd, Mead & Co., 1978. The first popular book on Egyptology by an Egyptologist and still the most entertaining. The author is also known as Elizabeth Peters and writes murder mysteries set in Egypt.

———. *Red Land, Black Land*. New York: Dodd, Mead & Co., 1978. The sequel to the above. Not a chronological history of Egypt, but it covers the high points.

Rice, Michael. *Egypt's Making*. London: Routledge, 1995. Detailed, authoritative telling of Egypt's early history from 5000–2000 B.C. Well illustrated.

Winlock, H. E. *The Rise and Fall of the Middle Kingdom in Thebes*. New York: Macmillan, 1947. An old work, so some of the details are wrong, but gives the best feeling for the period.

Art

Aldred, Cyril. *The Development of Ancient Egyptian Art.* London: Tiranti, 1965. An old standard combining three of the author's smaller works: *Old Kingdom, Middle Kingdom,* and *New Kingdom Art in Ancient Egypt.*

Bothmer, Bernard. *Egyptian Sculpture of the Late Period.* New York: The Brooklyn Museum, 1960. An exhibition catalog but also a standard work on the subject. Some of the pieces have recently been attributed to different dates, but the book is still an essential reference.

Kischkewitz, Hannelore. *Egyptian Art: Drawings and Paintings.* London: Hamlyn, 1989. Detailed discussions of how ancient artists produced Books of the Dead and tomb paintings.

————. *Egyptian Drawings.* London: Octopus, 1972. Covers much that is in the work above but does not provide as much detail.

Michalowski, Kazimierz. *Art of Ancient Egypt.* New York: Abrams, n.d. The most lavish history of Egyptian art. The illustrations are beautiful and the text important.

————. *Great Sculpture of Ancient Egypt.* New York: William Morrow, 1978. Excellent photos and brief discussions of masterpieces in the Egyptian Museum in Cairo.

Murray, Margaret Alice. *Egyptian Sculpture.* New York: Scribner's, 1930. A somewhat dated survey but contains a great illustration of a carving by a student of a hand with six fingers!

Peck, William H. *Egyptian Drawing.* London: Thames and Hudson, 1978. Good survey of the subject.

Rachewiltz, Boris de. *Egyptian Art.* New York: Viking, 1960. A good, solid work frequently found in used bookstores.

Russmann, Edna R. *Egyptian Sculpture: Cairo and Luxor.* Austin: University of Texas Press, 1989. Discussions of important pieces of sculpture. The text is by a great authority on the subject.

Scamuzzi, Ernesto. *Egyptian Art in the Egyptian Museum of Turin.* New York: Abrams, n.d. Presentation of a wonderful collection rarely seen by Americans.

Westendorf, Wolfhart. *Painting, Sculpture, and Architecture of Ancient Egypt.* New York: Abrams, 1968. Standard work with good illustrations. Frequently found in used bookstores.

Woldering, Imgard. *The Art of Ancient Egypt*. New York: Greystone Press, 1962. A good survey, strong on details of how art was produced.

Building and the Pyramids

Arnold, Dieter. *Building in Egypt*. Oxford: Oxford University Press, 1991. The definitive work and a great read.

Edwards, I. E. S. *The Pyramids of Egypt*. New York: Viking, 1985. An older work but still the best on the subject.

Fakhry, Ahmed. *The Pyramids*. Chicago: University of Chicago Press, 1969. A solid work by the Egyptian authority on the pyramids.

Habachi, Labib. *The Obelisks of Egypt*. New York: Scribner's, 1977. The best popular account of obelisks.

Lehner, Mark. *The Complete Pyramids*. London: Thames & Hudson, 1997.

Written by a real expert, this volume has wonderful computer-generated illustrations.

Mendelssohn, Kurt. *The Riddle of the Pyramids*. New York: Prager, 1974. Interesting reading, but the theory presented is probably false.

Noakes, Aubrey. *Cleopatra's Needles*. London: Wicherby, 1962. A popular account of the modern moving of obelisks.

Tompkins, Peter. *Secrets of the Great Pyramid*. New York: Harper & Roe, 1971. Good for illustrations and occult theories on the pyramid, but not much else.

Hieroglyphs

Collier, Mark, and Bill Manley. *How to Read Egyptian Hieroglyphs*. Berkeley: University of California Press, 1998. One of the best brief treatments that helps you learn by yourself.

Fischer, Henry. *Ancient Egyptian Calligraphy*. New York: Metropolitan Museum of Art, 1979. Delightful book that shows you how to draw the hieroglyphs. Great therapy!

Gardiner, Alan. *Egyptian Grammar*. Oxford: Griffith Institute, 1957. Still the definitive work; large, not easy to use by yourself, but wonderful.

Quirke, Stephen, and Carol Andrews. *The Rosetta Stone*. London: British Museum, 1988. Everything you want to know intelligently presented.

Kings and Queens

Arrian. *The Campaigns of Alexander the Great.* New York: Dorset, 1971. A primary source.

Bevan, Edwyn R. *The House of Ptolemy.* Chicago: Ares, reprint (original 1927), republished in 1968. An important source of information on the period and the Ptolemies.

Bianchi, Robert. *Cleopatra's Egypt.* New York: Brooklyn Museum, 1988. Spectacular exhibition catalogue of art from the time of Cleopatra. Also includes much useful historical information.

Bradford, Ernle. *Cleopatra.* New York: Harcourt Brace, 1972. A detailed but readable biography.

Brier, Bob. *The Murder of Tutankhamen.* New York: Putnam's, 1998. Theory that the boy-king was killed but also presents historical background.

Desmond, Alice Curtis. *Cleopatra's Children.* New York: Dodd, 1971. The only work on what happened to Cleo's kids. Readable and well researched.

Foreman, Laura. *Cleopatra's Palace.* New York: Random House, 1999. A beautiful book tied to a television special but better than the program.

Fox, Robin Lane. *Alexander the Great.* New York: Dial, 1974. A readable, accurate biography.

Freed, Rita A. *Ramses the Great.* Boston: Boston Museum of Science, 1987. An exhibition catalogue but with a concise history of Ramses and good photographs of objects from the period.

George, Margaret. *Memoirs of Cleopatra.* New York: St. Martin's Press, 1997. A monumental, historically accurate fictional biography of Cleopatra. Wonderful.

Grant, Michael. *Cleopatra.* New York: Simon and Schuster, 1972. Solid biography of the last queen of Egypt.

———. *From Alexander to Cleopatra.* New York: Scribner's, 1982. Rich background to the lives of the kings and queens of the Greek period.

Hughes-Hallett, Lucy. *Cleopatra.* New York, Harper, 1990. More a social history of how Cleopatra was viewed than a biography. Quite interesting.

Kitchen, K. A. *Pharaoh Triumphant: The Life and Times of Ramses II*. Cairo: American University in Cairo Press, 1982. The definitive work by the leading Ramses scholar. Highly readable.

Lindsay, Jack. *Cleopatra*. New York: Coward McCann, 1970. Readable, literary type of biography, sans footnotes.

Tyldesley, Joyce. *Hatshepsut*. New York: Viking, 1996. The most recent and best biography of the female pharaoh.

Medicine

Breasted, James Henry. *The Edwin Smith Surgical Papyrus*. Chicago: University of Chicago Press, 1930. Hieroglyphs and translation of a papyrus that told physicians how to treat trauma. Fascinating.

Bryan, Cyril P. *Ancient Egyptian Medicine—Papyrus Ebers*. Chicago: Ares, 1974. Translation of a papyrus that includes magical/pharmacological treatments for many ailments.

Estes, J. Worth. *The Medical Skills of Ancient Egypt*. Canton: Science History Publications, 1993. Useful.

Ghalioungui, Paul. *The House of Life*. Amsterdam: Ben Israel, 1973. Written by an Egyptologist/physician, this is one of the best overviews of the medical practice in ancient Egypt.

Nunn, John F. *Ancient Egyptian Medicine*. London: British Museum, 1996. The most recent and best work on the subject. Illustrated.

Mummies

Brier, Bob. *Egyptian Mummies*. New York: William Morrow, 1994. The basic survey of the subject.

Budge, E. A. Wallis. *The Mummy*. New York: Causeway, 1974. Reprint of a 100-year-old classic. Much is outdated but good for hieroglyphic spells associated with mummification.

Cockburn, Aidan, et al. *Mummies, Disease and Ancient Cultures*. Cambridge: Cambridge University Press, 1998. Mummies around the world but much on Egypt, focusing on high-tech paleopathology.

El Mahdy, Christine. *Mummies, Myth and Magic*. London: Thames & Hudson, 1989. Popular survey with interesting illustrations but too many errors to be trusted.

Ikram, Salima, and Aidan Dodson. *The Mummy in Ancient Egypt*. London: Thames & Hudson, 1998. Wonderfully illustrated survey of funerary practices. Much on coffins, canopic chests, and so on.

Partridge, Robert B. *Faces of Pharaohs*. London: Rubicon, 1994. Photos of all the royal mummies and their coffins with brief descriptions. Useful for reference.

Pettigrew, Thomas J. *A History of Egyptian Mummies*. Los Angeles: North American Archives, n.d. Reprint of 1834 work by the greatest mummy unroller of all times. Gives many references of ancient comments on mummification.

Smith, G. Elliot, and Warren R. Dawson. *Egyptian Mummies*. London: Kegan Paul, 1991. Reprint of the 1924 work that was the basic book on the subject for years. Still useful.

Religion

Frankfort, H. *Ancient Egyptian Religion*. New York: Columbia University Press, 1948. A fundamental work on the topic but very dated.

Hornung, Erick. *Conceptions of God in Ancient Egypt*. Ithaca: Cornell University Press, 1985. Excellent essays but a bit technical.

Morentz, Sigfried. *Egyptian Religion*. Ithaca: Cornell University Press, 1973. A solid work.

Akhenaten and the Amarna Period

Aldred, Cyril. *Akhenaten, King of Egypt*. London: Thames & Hudson, 1988. One of the two or three basic works on the subject by a highly respected Amarna scholar.

———. *Akhenaten and Nefertiti*. New York: Brooklyn Museum, 1973. An exhibition catalogue that includes important information on the subject.

Anon. *Amarna Letters*, 3 vols. San Francisco: KMT Communications, 1991–1994. Anthologies of essays by various scholars. Both readable and informative.

Arnold, Dorothea. *The Royal Women of Amarna*. New York: Metropolitan Museum of Art, 1997. Essays by various scholars on the different women of the Amarna period. Beautiful illustrations, important text.

Desroches-Noblecourt, Christiane. *Tutankhamen*. New York: New York Graphic Society, 1963. Some unusual theories but gives a wonderful feeling of the period.

Kozloff, Arielle P., and Betsy M. Bryan. *Egypt's Dazzling Sun*. A beautifully illustrated exhibition catalogue but far more, including the best history of Amenhotep III available.

Moran, William. *The Amarna Letters*. Baltimore: Johns Hopkins University Press, 1992. Translations of the cuneiform letters written to Akhenaten from abroad. Shows Egypt declining.

Murnane, William J. *Texts from the Amarna Period in Egypt*. Atlanta: Scholars Press, 1995. Translations of all the major Egyptian documents from the period. An important research tool and fascinating.

———, and Charles C. Van Siclen III. *The Boundary Stelae of Akhenaten*. London: Kegan-Paul, 1993. Translations of all the boundary markers of Akhenaten's city in the desert.

Redford, D. B. *Akhenaten, the Heretic King*. Princeton: Princeton University Press, 1984. An important work by the man who excavated Akhenaten's temples at Karnak and grew to hate the king!

Reeves, Nicholas. *The Complete Tutankhamen*. London: Thames & Hudson, 1990. It really is complete! (With wonderful illustrations.)

———, and John H. Taylor. *Howard Carter Before Tutankhamen*. New York: Abrams, 1992. Gives a detailed account of Carter's career leading up to the discovery of Tutankhamen's tomb.

Smith, Ray Winfield, and Donald B. Redford. *The Akhenaten Temple Project*. Warminster: Aris & Phillips, 1976. The attempt to reconstruct Akhenaten's Karnak temples on paper with the aid of a computer.

Velikovsky, Immannuel. *Oedipus and Akhenaten*. New York: Doubleday, 1960. A crazy theory that Akhenaten was the Greek King Oedipus, but it is interesting to see how the case is presented.

Daily Life

Erman, Adolf. *Life in Ancient Egypt*. New York: Dover, 1971. Reprint of a 100-year-old work but still useful for its illustrations of the details of the lives of the ancient Egyptians.

Maspero, Gaston C. C. *Life in Ancient Egypt and Assyria*. New York: Unger, 1971. Reprint of a 100-year-old work but useful.

Wilkinson, J. Gardner. *The Ancient Egyptians: Their Lives and Customs*. New York: Crescent Books, 1988. Reprint of a 100-year-old work that is dated in some of its conclusions but includes hundreds of wonderful line drawings from the tombs of the nobles at Thebes.

Miscellaneous

Bietak, Manfred. *Avaris, The Capital of the Hyksos*. London: British Museum, 1996. Excavation report that shows how difficult it is to reconstruct the history of the Hyksos.

Brier, Bob. *Ancient Egyptian Magic*. New York: Morrow, 1980. A broad survey of magical practices.

———. *The Glory of Ancient Egypt*. Millwood: Kraus Reprint Co., 1988. Much information on Napoleon's Egyptian campaign and the *Description de l'Egypte*.

Budge, Wallis. *Egyptian Magic*. New York: University Books, n.d. Reprint of an 1899 work but still contains some useful information.

Frerichs, Ernest, and Leonard Lesko. *Exodus, the Egyptian Evidence*. Winona Lake: Eisenbrauns, 1997. A small book of essays by experts on both sides of the Exodus question.

Herold, J. Christopher. *Bonaparte in Egypt*. New York: Harper, 1962. The author hates Bonaparte, but the book is a wonderful read with great information.

Sandars, N. K. *The Sea Peoples*. London: Thames & Hudson, 1978. One of the few books on this important subject.

Societies

The Amarna Research Foundation, Inc., 6082 E. Loyola Place, Aurora, CO 80013. Interested in all aspects of the Amarna period, the foundation's activities center on the current excavations at Amarna headed by Dr. Barry Kemp. A newsletter is published.

American Research Center in Egypt (ARCE), Emory University, West Campus, 1256 Briarcliff Road, NE, Building A, Suite 423W, Atlanta, Georgia, 30306. Organization of professional Egyptologists and laymen interested in all aspects of Egypt, including Coptic and Islamic. An annual conference is held and a journal (*JARCE*) is published. The following chapters sponsor lectures by Egyptologists and publish newsletters.

North Texas Chapter: P.O. Box 38642, Dallas, TX 57238

Southern California Chapter: 3460 South Broadway, Los Angeles, CA 90007.

Northern California Chapter: P.O. Box 11352, Berkeley, CA, 94712.

Washington, D.C. Chapter: 3737 Fessenden Street NW, Washington, D.C., 20016.

Ancient Egypt Studies Association (AESA), 7110 S.E. 29th Avenue, Portland, Oregon, 97202. A group of interested laypersons and professionals with regular meetings, lectures, and a newsletter.

Egypt Exploration Society (EES), 3 Doughty Mews, London WC1N 2PG, London, England. Publishes the *Journal of Egyptian Archaeology*, as well as a glossy magazine, *Egyptian Archaeology*, and sponsors several lectures in London each year.

Egyptian Study Society (ESS), Denver Museum of Natural History, 2001 Colorado Boulevard, Denver, CO, 80205. Another group of interested laypersons and professionals with meetings, lectures, and a newsletter.

Egyptological Seminar of New York (ESNY), c/o Dag Bergman, 45 Clara St., Brooklyn, NY 11218. Sponsors lectures in New York by visiting Egyptologists and publishes a journal, *Bulletin of the Egyptological Seminar of New York (BES)*, and a newsletter.

KMT: A Modern Journal of Ancient Egypt, Dept. G, P.O. Box 1475, Sebastopol, CA 95473. The journal publishes articles on culture, history, personalities, arts, and monuments of ancient Egypt.

Oriental Institute, University of Chicago, 1155 East 58 St., Chicago, IL 60637. Sponsors lectures in Chicago and programs for children and has a correspondence course in hieroglyphs. A newsletter is published, as well as an annual report of the Institute's activities.

Notes

Notes